CHE GUEVARA

His Revolutionary Legacy

CHE GUEVARA

His Revolutionary Legacy

Olivier Besancenot
Michael Löwy

translated by
James Membrez

AAKAR

Che Guevara: His Revolutionary Legacy
Olivier Besancenot and Michael Löwy

First Published in India, 2009
Reprinted 2017
Reprinted 2021
Reprinted 2024

ISBN 978-93-5002-016-6

Published in agreement with Monthly Review Press, New York for publication and sale only in South Asia.

Published by
AAKAR BOOKS
28 E Pocket IV, Mayur Vihar Phase I
Delhi 110 091, India
www.aakarbooks.com

Printed at
D.K. Fine Art Press, Delhi

CONTENTS

Introduction 7

One Night, Somewhere in Bolivia 11

1. A Marxist Humanism 29

2. Socialist Revolution or Caricature of Revolution 47

3. In Search of a New Model of Socialism 65

4. The Guevarist Heritage in Latin America 79

5. From Internationalism to Alterglobalism,
from the Tricontinental to the Intercontinental 93

Appendix
Che: A Thinker of Acts by Daniel Bensaïd 111
Concerning Ernesto Che Guevara
by Subcomandante Marcos 119

Chronology of Important Dates 121

Notes 125

Bibliography 135

Index 139

Introduction

Ernesto Guevara de la Serna, Argentine doctor who became Minister of Industry in Cuba, fell in combat against the military dictatorship in Bolivia on October 8, 1967. There are a large number of biographies on Che. We have decided to focus on his ideas, values, analyses, proposals, and dreams. Certainly he was a combatant who wielded the pen as easily as the gun. But for what cause did he fight? How did he view the struggle of the people of Latin America and the entire world for their liberation? What image did he have of socialism, of the "new man," of a society finally freed from the capitalist nightmare? These are the questions that concern us in this book; we make no pretense of offering the definitive answers.

Ernesto "Che" Guevara was not a saint, a superman, or an infallible leader: he was a man like others. He had strengths and weaknesses, insights and blind spots; he made mistakes and blunders. But he had a rare quality among political actors: a consistency between his words and acts, his ideas and practice, his thought and action. From this point of view, he was exceptional. This accounts for much of the attraction he holds, even today, for numerous people—notably youth—throughout the world.

Guevara was a Marxist revolutionary and an uncompromising opponent of the people-crushing machine of imperialism and the inherently perverted system of capitalism. His Marxism is a result of his *ad hoc* readings, encounters, and experiences. He cannot easily be pigeonholed into any of the usual compartments. Beginning in the 1950s, he continued to deepen his political thinking, developing an approach that was unique to him, which the assassins of the Bolivian dictatorship ended prematurely. We are going to try to grasp the movement and the evolution of his political thought.

The authors of this book belong to two different generations, and we have different interpretations and approaches to Che's work. But our approaches, far from being contradictory, have turned out to be complementary and convergent. The result of our work is neither a "manual of Guevarism" nor an imaginary systematization of a largely unsystematic and constantly changing work. Rather, it is, above all, an attempt to demonstrate the contribution that Guevara makes to socialism of the twenty-first century.

We are not offering a nostalgic look at Che's thought. On the contrary, revisiting his ideas, forty years after his death, makes it possible to grasp their passionate relevance for the work of Marxist renewal and the radical cultural and political reform undertaken by those who have not abandoned the attempt to construct an alternative to capitalism.

Certainly, the world in which we live no longer appears to have much in common with the world from before 1967. When the Berlin Wall fell in 1989, it marked the beginning of a new era. Yet far from ending in the advent of socialism with a human face, the long-awaited fall of the USSR and its brother countries ultimately led to the establishment of an unrestrained capitalism. The Cold War gave way to hot, petroleum-motivated wars, as reflected in the two recent wars led by the United States against Iraq. East and West no longer confront each other directly and have reconciled on the back of the countries of the South, under the approving eye of the dollar god. Other walls are being built: from the circuitous Israeli walls in Palestine to the borders of the United States and Europe, which have become imperial fortresses that pillage the wealth of the third world with no thought given to sharing the smallest crumb. In brief, the entire world has been subjected to the total rule of a ferocious and brutal market economy.

Since 1990, capitalism, celebrated by the partisans of neoliberalism, is presented as the unsurpassable horizon of humanity and the last stage of History. All political currents that dare to defy it are suspected of potential "totalitarianism," even if some those currents denounced, well before the ideologues of neoliberalism, the totalitarian brutalities of Stalinism. Like an eternal burden, the opponents of capitalism have been condemned to carry the awful consequences of a dictatorial and murderous system that they had fiercely fought at the price of many sacrifices and destroyed lives in the purges and gulags. Guevarists, Trotskyists, libertarians, revolutionary syndicalists, radical third worldists, and anti-Stalinist communists have all been sent back to the dock to appear before the prosecutors of "really-existing" capitalism in the great trial of communism. This is a trial that places executioners and victims, revolutionaries and counter-revolutionaries side by side. Not to accept capitalism is a crime in itself.

And then, despite itself, contemporary capitalism witnessed a new antidote to its own poison. In the wake of poverty, famine, exploitation, wars, and environmental disasters, capitalist globalization gave rise to new struggles of resistance and, consequently, new hopes. It is at the heart of this other America and on the well-marked path of Che's struggles that the star of the human adventure began to shine again. It sparkled all the more brightly since the night, at that time, was particularly dark. January 1, 1994, in southeast Mexico, in Chiapas, the Zapatista peasants took up arms to say "*¡Ya basta!*" to the new world order. In December 1995, in France, the first large revolt against neoliberalism sounded the renewal of social struggle.

Since then, a phrase continues to ring out: "Another world is possible." This urgent cry voiced by the people was heard during the general strikes in Europe and Asia; it burst forth from the insurrectional movements in Latin America, in Venezuela, Argentina, Bolivia and Ecuador. It continues to be heard in the social forums of the alterglobalization movements.

Currently, capitalism is still the great winner. It flaunts itself with even more arrogance since there is no credible political alternative. The consequences of Stalinism weigh heavily on the socialist idea. It is not just the millions of deaths. It has discredited for an entire generation the idea that a functional system other than capitalism could be established. However, imagination is reclaiming its rights and gradually rising from the ashes. Within this new ideological turmoil in search of egalitarian, democratic, and anti-bureaucratic solutions, Che's thought is an inexhaustible source of inspiration. Ready-made models do not exist. The great revolutions must once again be assessed: from the Paris Commune in 1871 to the Latin American revolutions of the 1960s and 1970s, as well as the Russian Revolution of October 1917 and the Spanish Revolution of 1936. Revolutionaries must, with a critical eye, draw from these episodes adequate democratic solutions. They must also learn again that the multitude of the exploited and oppressed, united and in solidarity, is capable of taking its destiny in hand if it decides to do so. No revolutionary current, not Guevarist, Trotskyist, or libertarian, can alone presume to incarnate the synthesis of these experiences.

Today, this critical reexamination concerns the entirety of the Left and the workers' movement. Recall that, without these revolutions, without these ruptures, without these oppositional movements, our social gains would be quite paltry. The specter of a revolution in France, in 1936, at the Liberation, or in May 1968 seems to have been more effective than leftist governments in obtaining elementary social rights: public services, social security, or paid vacations. Paid vacations never figured in the electoral program of the Popular Front. They were obtained because our ancestors paralyzed and blockaded the country by massively occupying their workplaces. The owners, preferring to lose money rather than their power in society, were thus forced to give way.

The great project to build twenty-first century socialism has begun. We do not have ready answers for every question. Still, some paths of thinking are opening before us, and those of the past have not all become dead-ends. Many claim that the flame of our hopes was extinguished with the demise of the tragic and bloody experience known as "real socialism." We respond: an ember still burns—the communism of Che Guevara.

One Night, Somewhere in Bolivia

He falls to the ground, crushed under the weight of his backpack. Once seated, he takes off the pack with difficulty, opens it, and rummages inside, searching for his invaluable travel diary, which is not immediately obvious among all his things. First, he pushes aside the geographical maps that he has regularly annotated with crayons during these last few months on the march. The forest through which he and his comrades are laboriously moving is virgin, unexplored, and obviously poorly recorded. The mountains, ravines, and paths are impassable. The jungle is hostile, the rain incessant, sometimes interspersed with a blazing sun. Mosquitoes and ticks tirelessly pursue their curious procession. Each of them has had to learn how to live with these insects. Like everyone here, he is at the end of his strength, hungry, thirsty, scrawny, and sick, even if he seeks to hide it as much as he can. He has barely recovered from the stomach upset and vomiting that has been torturing him for more than a week. His asthma has not relented. In fact, it would not be surprising if the opposite were true in these extreme conditions. He was almost born with the condition.

Too young then to remember it, his mother had told him how this suffocating, daily companion had suddenly appeared. Everything had begun under the best auspices. Well taken care of since his birth at Rosario de Santa Fe, in Argentina, "Tété" knew only, until two years of age, the love of his devoted and cultivated mother, Celia, and the affection of his father, Ernesto, a construction engineer. Then, the pneumonia that he had contracted one morning in May 1930, in the icy waters of a river, had degenerated into chronic asthma. Weakened by this terrible handicap, he had taken on the habit of occupying himself on long days of pain and rest with reading numerous books. When strong enough, his health benefited from engaging in intense sports, such as swimming, rugby, and soccer.

Asthmatic from the very beginning, he wanders today in Bolivia, deprived of medications. He could not say, exactly, if it is the illness or the medicine that he finds the most vexing. In fact, helping his companions, or even his enemies, and treating the peasants have become a habit with him, almost a mission. Mechanically verifying the absence of tablets, injection needles, and a first-aid kit in his bag, he is reassured upon finding his *bombilla* of *maté*—his Argentine tea, a magic potion and umbilical cord that, fifteen years after leaving, still connects him to his birthplace.

At the beginning of 1947, he had decided to become a doctor, motivated by his own illness and by his desire to help his fellow human beings. His medical studies had driven him to move to Buenos Aires and to leave his parents, then living in Alta Gracia, at the foot of the Andes. Medicine had given him wings. In the summer of 1948, recently graduated and astride a motorcycle specially outfitted for the occasion, he had joined his friend, Alberto Granado, at the leper colony in San Francisco del Chañar. Eight hundred and fifty kilómeters they traveled, a small trip around the world. His world had become much larger since then: not only Argentina, but also Chile, Peru, Bolivia, Colombia, Guatemala, Mexico, then Cuba, Egypt, Algeria, Yugoslavia, China, the USSR, Congo, and many other countries. Travel had broadened his mind, as well as his consciousness. Inequality and injustice had always appalled him. Despite coming from a middle-class background, he kept a memory of his childhood play companions, poor and destitute, like the Indian families, packed into makeshift housing. His father had organized a progressive support committee for the Spanish Republic in 1937. But his father had a more cautious assessment of the transformation of the family home into a *casa del pueblo* (house of the people), open to all these poor children.

But the events that truly founded his commitment were the ones he experienced in the course of his two tours of Latin America. He had made his first trip with Granado, his accomplice, on an old Norton 500 cc, *La Poderosa II*, "The Powerful One." Time had not erased these memories, as if their departure, December 29, 1951, had just happened yesterday. How could he forget the outrage he had experienced when faced with the sufferings of the peasants, deprived of land because of the stranglehold of the *latifundistas* over agriculture? The inequalities were glaring along the road that leads from Argentina to Venezuela, crossing neglected regions and working class neighborhoods of Chile, Peru, and Colombia. On the one hand, there was the luxury of the wealthy seaside resort of Miramar, in Argentina, which had been the site of the initial events of their journey. They had remained at Miramar for some time, accepting the loving welcome of his girlfriend, Chichina. On the other hand, there was the poverty of millions of Latin Americans. He, "Fuser," a name given to him by Granado—from "*furibondo* de la Serna"—had been moved by a deep anger in Chile, at Chuquicamata, the aptly named "red mountain" in the indigenous language. Outraged and ashamed at the sight of the exploitation of copper miners by a cynical and contemptuous North American company, the Argentine had then understood that Latin America was only one of the "properties of United Fruit," as he had written to his aunt Beatriz in reference to the Yankee system. He, the white man, had had to admit, at the summit of Machu Picchu, that the Indians of the Andes had never stopped struggling against the destruction of their civilization. He, the young man who had bought a ticket for the school of adventure, discovered, as a revelation, the hidden history of the liberation movements tacitly linking the struggles of Tupac Amaru in 1745 to those of Simón Bolívar in 1825. This was a still smoldering history that was going to seize and hold the young adventurer as he gradually became a fighter in the ongoing battle against the conquistadors, past and present. Finally, he, the apprentice doctor, had come to understand at the leper colony of San Pablo, in Peru, that medicine was not an end in itself, but, all the same, it was time to master it more quickly in order to move into action and do battle under new horizons. Upon his return to Argentina, he had then passed, in record time. his ten examinations and received a diploma in medicine. The end of this first journey of seven months, however, was not a farewell to the road.

Lost in his thoughts, his eyes immersed in the darkness of the night, he lightly shakes his head. He still remembers his mother's face on the platform of the station, July 7, 1953, worried to see him leaving again. Her face clouded over even more when, through the window of the train, he could not stop himself from yelling: "Thus goes a soldier of America!"

This second trip also had remained engraved in his memory. The hitchhiking, the boat, and his bloody feet had this time led his steps onto the path that gradually transforms revolt into the desire for revolution. They had first led him into the impoverished neighborhoods of La Paz. He had interfered in Bolivian government offices, where scenes of humiliation towards the Indians were an ordinary occurrence. He had stopped at the intoxicating landscapes of Lake Titicaca and Machu Picchu, where the eternal shadow of the pre-Columbian civilizations hangs. He had ended his trip in San José, Costa Rica, having passed through Ecuador, Nicaragua, and Panama. There, he had good political discussions with numerous Latin American political exiles, particularly with Cubans. Also, as far as he remembers, this was the first time he had heard the name of a certain Fidel Castro Ruz mentioned. He was a student leader, imprisoned with his comrades since they had attacked a barracks on July 26, 1953, in Santiago, Cuba, in a struggle against the Batista dictatorship. In Guatemala, he had decided to give himself over to "improving himself and becoming this authentic revolutionary" whose merits he had praised to his aunt.

At the beginning of 1954, Guatemala had just experienced a revolution that was nipped in the bud. The government of Colonel Jacobo Arbenz had begun a courageous agrarian reform, favorable to the Guatemalan peasants. This reform, in fact, damaged the interests of the North American fruit companies, omnipresent for decades in the country. The people's raised hopes had soon been destroyed in the flames of American bombardments and had been betrayed by the powerlessness of Arbenz, who had laid down his arms without allowing the people to put up resistance to the military *coup d'état.*

Thirteen years later, these powerful memories still leave him with a bitter taste. But the bitterness will not erase the happy moments of this part of his life. Guatemala had also been the place where he met Hilda, his first wife. Hildita, now grown, was born from their love. Guatemala had also prompted meetings with militants, such as Ñico López, a pro-Castro Cuban exiled after the failed attack on the Moncada Barracks, and who had contaminated him with the virus of the Cuban Revolution. He had again encountered this same Ñico López, since killed in combat in Cuba, several months later in Mexico, place of exile for Guatemalan refugees. The honeymoon with Hilda had not lasted long. One evening in July 1955, with López acting as intermediary, he met Fidel for the first time. He would never forget their discussion, which lasted all night. At dawn, he knew he would be a combatant in the Cuban Revolution.

He removes from his pack the codebooks that allow the decryption of coded messages transmitted by transistor. But, in reality, he no longer communicates much with Cuba, since, for several weeks, he can no longer send any messages, only receive them. The radio is the last link connecting him and his men to the outside. Some time earlier, the urban support network for the guerillas was permanently decapitated with the arrest of Loyola Guzmán, treasurer of the ELN, the National Liberation Army. With his incarceration, the central piece of the rear support system disappeared. A true disaster, because the movement in the cities provided fresh supplies and logistics and carried out vital political activity with the working class. And, barely an hour ago, the radio announced again that 250 soldiers were on the point of encircling them. Fine, but this is not the first time that he has heard such announcements.

He looks at the moon. Small, yet it clearly shines on those who, for months, travel through the night. Around him, the men started sleeping as soon as they stopped walking. The night is particularly cold. Everyone is covered with a jacket. So is he. His old shirt without the buttons would not suffice. He hesitates to put on his hood. His cap with the earflaps, colored green-bronze, should be sufficient. He no longer takes it off; he wears it night and day.

He had bought this cap in Paris in the course of one of his numerous stops between Cuba and La Paz. Traveling a circuitous route had allowed him to cover his tracks and shake off the international authorities, who are unhappy with having lost track of him since his departure from Cuba. He thus arrived incognito in Bolivia on November 3, 1966. He still remembers his passport number, since he had had to learn his new identity by heart: 130748. The passport was in the name of a certain Adolfo Mena Gonzáles, a Uruguayan sociologist—a curious person, this sociologist. Bald, wearing large glasses, he had made a last visit to his family in Cuba under the name of Ramon. His second wife, Aleida, with whom he had fallen in love during the Cuban guerilla war, had played the game by welcoming her disguised husband before their children, unconcerned. Aleidita, his daughter, however, could not be prevented from having doubts about this alleged Spaniard who too much resembled an Argentine.

This evening, these months of separation from his family weigh heavily on him. He touches, without looking at it, the photo of his wife and children that he carefully keeps in his pocket.

Also in Paris, he had bought his pipe, and at a high price. He smiles inside on remembering the scene at Orly Airport. Just when he was ready to light the pipe that he had already stuffed, the merchant in the store had subdued his enthusiasm by telling him the exorbitant price. The story could have ended in a scene if Pacho, alias Alberto Fernández, had not settled the bill from his pocket, uncomfortable at the anger of señor Mena.

Pacho sleeps deeply, leaning against his pack. Mechanically tamping down the tobacco in his pipe, he does not take his eyes off him. He regrets not having saved one of the Cuban cigars he likes so much, the ones that he smoked on important occasions. The important occasions are rather infrequent now. Anyhow, given the proximity of the military troops, it would be pure folly to light a cigar that, while burning, would certainly lead to their being found.

Pipe in his mouth, he rummages again in his bag and finally locates his fine notebook. His left hand, cut on the back, caresses the green cover of the notebook in which he regularly copies poems by Neruda, León Felipe, and Guillén. Under the stack are found the campaign diaries of his comrades, which he keeps for security. Pombo, Pacho, Rolando, Braulio, and Moro recount the daily occurrences of their Bolivian odyssey since November 7, 1966.

Then he picks up his own diary, a red one. On the back of the cover is affixed a label that reads: "Carl Klippel—Kaiserstrasse, 75—Frankfurt." His gaze stops briefly on the first page that he had opened with an invitation as urgent as his writing: "Today a new step begins!"

But what step? To be frank, he had long hesitated over the destination of his guerilla nucleus. He was convinced of the necessity of forming a rear base at the center of Latin America, of training several armed movements, in Peru, Bolivia, Argentina, Chile, Paraguay, and Brazil. His plan was that the Andes Mountains would become the Sierra Maestra—the initial focus for the armed struggle in Cuba—for all of Latin America. His intention was not to copy the Cuban model exactly, but consisted more of fermenting a conflict akin to the one in Vietnam and thereby opening a second front of fighting against the Yankees. Moreover, he had never hidden that objective and had not said anything different in his official speeches, when he was in the Cuban government. He had proclaimed to the whole world his personal intention to fight to the death against imperialism by spreading the revolution, leaving Soviet tutelage behind. That had been the sense of his plea before the UN on December 9, 1964, and then of his indictment presented in Algiers on February 15, 1965. This was also the sense of the message that the Cuban journal *Granma* had published last April 17. This appeal, this "cry of war against imperialism," was intended for all the peoples of America, Asia, and Africa. Thousands of miles from Cuba, he had heard his text read on the radio, perched in a tree in Bolivia. His phrase "create two, three, many Vietnams," he knew, must have irritated the White House and chilled the Kremlin. Igniting new embers was a necessity without which the Cuban flame itself would end up suffocating under the leaden weight of a nascent bureaucracy.

Throughout these reflections, he continues to leaf through the pages of the notebook.

To begin a new step also responded to a need that he had felt individually after having fought the dictatorship and leading the Cuban Revolution from 1956 to 1965, for almost ten years. However this new step was not only to allow him to continue his "wandering through the world." This was a guarantee that he had demanded of Fidel, at the time of their meeting, before becoming involved in the Cuban liberation. This step also had another function: to efface the unhappy episode of the Congo. Obviously, the seven months of combat that he had spent supporting the guerilla war of Laurent-Désiré Kabila had not been pointless. There were, originally, even good reasons to believe in it. The revolutionary movements of the Congolese National Council had requested such support, after the assassination of progressive and pro-independence prime minister Patrice Lumumba in January 1961 by the troops of Moïse Tshombe. Fidel himself, unlike the Bolivian project, was favorable to it. Under the code name "Tatu" (the Swahili word for the number three), he had invested one year in this clandestine adventure in the Congo. One year, as he once said, "where we were nowhere in the eyes of the world."

Too many obstacles had arisen: differences in culture and language, the lack of preparedness for combat on the part of the African groups. He, the White Man, even surrounded by his garrison of Black Cubans, moved politically and psychologically in a universe of concerns, points of reference, usages, customs, even local superstitions, far from anything familiar. The use of *dawa*, a magic potion distributed by a sorcerer to the soldiers and alleged to make them invulnerable to bullets, had not made him smile for long. But beyond all that, what had given rise to the most frustration in the man of action was to be paralyzed while awaiting instructions, which proved as unusual as the appearances of Kabila. He had drawn a definite lesson from this experience: in order to be effective, the next step had to occur militarily under his sole command, so that he would no longer have to depend on anyone. His intransigence on the subject had allowed the Bolivian Communist Party to disguise political divergences within the leadership with the strategic question of armed struggle: the party insisted on the illegitimacy of a non-Bolivian leading an insurrection on Bolivian territory. This is one of the reasons why he would have much preferred fighting in his home country, Argentina.

Between his last public appearance in Cuba, on March 22, 1965, during a conference on Africa at the Ministry of Industry, and his clandestine entry into Bolivia at the beginning of November 1966, more than a year had passed. Before arriving in Bolivia, he had to wait five long months secretly in the solitude of Prague. Here, Che had succeeded in coming to terms with the Congolese failure in which he had experienced great setbacks and defeats, culminating in a retreat at the end of 1965. In Prague, he had taken the time to revive the scenário, which he had been continually working on since the summer of 1963, concerning the possibility of launching the struggle from Peru, Bolivia, and Argentina. He had closely followed the movements of the survivors of a Peruvian guerilla column, refugees in La Paz since May 1963. He had commissioned José María Tamayo, Cuban captain in Bolivia since July of the same year, to establish contacts with the initial networks. He was involved in the creation of the EGP, the Guerilla Army of the People, which, under the command of his friend, the journalist Jorge Masetti, had begun its activity in Argentina in September 1963. Broken up in April 1964, the guerilla war of his dead friend had sounded the knell of a personal project in Argentina. Bolivia was, then, necessary as the combat front as such and also as the rear base of a continental armed movement. He had then dispatched Tania, a former translator whom he had met in Moscow and who belonged to the Cuban secret services, to infiltrate La Paz high society.

He reaches an empty page of his notebook, on the top of which he writes the date: October 7, 1967. He rejects the internal doubts that he senses rising in him and convinces himself quickly that the Bolivian mission is the first step, not the last. Although the recent material and military difficulties are beginning to worry him, he still entertains the secret hope of pushing the affair further. And if it were necessary to die as a result, as he confided to Ulises Estrado, agent of the Cuban Interior Ministry with him in Prague, he hoped that it would be "with at least a small piece of his foot in Argentina."

For the moment, his feet are in Bolivia and they are a sad sight. A month ago, while crossing a stream, he lost his shoes. His lace and rope sandals, even with three pairs of socks, offer little protection against brambles and roots and are no protection against the cold. Pencil in hand, beginning to write, he rereads what he wrote the day before: ". . . Chilean radio reports censored news to the effect that there are 1850 men in the area on our tails." Who believes it, in any case? He, chess player before the Eternal, moves in risky territory where he cannot see the opponent move his pawns. One thing is certain: for the last week, there have been only seventeen guerillas left to fight. Too many friends have fallen. The entire rear guard was destroyed at the end of August, including Tania, Acuña, and Machin, as well as those companions always close to him: his guard Coco, several days ago, San Luis, his messenger since Column Four in the Sierra Maestra, and then Collo, whom he loved as his son. Instinctively, he looks at his second watch, the one that Collo gave him before he died: 2:30—and he still can't sleep.

After all, there were never hundreds in his troop; at its strongest, only fifty. Further, there were only seventeen belonging to the Cuban commandos, selected and secretly trained for three months on the property of Pinar del Río, from the middle of July to the middle of October 1966. Anyway, there were only seventeen left to fire the shot against Batista, after the wreck of their boat, the *Granma*, on which they had originally embarked with eighty-two.

He knows that his own morale has an effect on that of the group. He starts to write: "Eleven months since our inauguration as guerillas; the day was being spent without complications, even bucolically, until 12:30 when an old woman shepherding her goats came into the canyon where we had camped and it was necessary to apprehend her. The woman gave no truthful news about the soldiers, saying that she didn't know anything, as it was a long time since she had gone there. She only gave information about the roads; and, according to her report, it shows that we are approximately one league from Higueras and another from Jaguey and about two from Pucara. At 17:30, Inti, Aniceto, and Pablito went to the old woman's house where she has two daughters, one crippled and the other half-dwarfed. Fifty pesos were given to her with the request that she not say a word, but with little hope that she would keep her promise."

He pauses on these words and considers that the isolation from which they suffer does not come only from the absence of an urban network or the recent successes of the army, which had found their supplies hidden in the caves around their rear base, the farm at Ñancahuasú. Their isolation comes from the fear, sometimes the hostility, of the peasant population, which flees from them, fearing the guerilla war. He knows that they are moving in an area favorable to providing information to the army. In the Sierra Maestra, the peasants supported the guerilla war. He cared for them, taught them to read and write, educated them, politicized them, and loved them. Perhaps the timid agrarian reform from which they benefited here explains the difficulties in establishing a strong relationship. Perhaps the force of this Bolivian region, the fact that it is almost uninhabited, is turning against them. Had he not written, in his assessment of the preceding month, that the "most important task is to begin searching for more favorable areas"?

The choice of Ñancahuasú had been made in October 1966, several days before his arrival, in great haste. By sending Tamayo from Prague to Bolivia again, he was counting on creating a little order before his arrival. But the disagreements among the different revolutionary currents inevitably continued. The recruits of the Maoist guerilla group of his namesake, Moïse Guevara, were kept waiting and once they had been put in position, they turned out to be very weak politically: a veritable breeding ground of potential deserters and informers. Above all, the two-sided discourse of the Bolivian Communist Party leadership on armed struggle, which listened only to its Soviet master, was, as he suspected, rapidly transformed into the pure and simple abandonment of his group. It seemed that the favorable echo the guerilla war had initially encountered in the population, and which continued to be true, was continually frustrated because of the failure of a sufficiently organized urban network to tap into it. Worse, the San Juan massacre, last June 24, had not provoked any unified reaction from the political parties, even though the army had killed eighty-seven miners only because their union supported the guerilla war.

This makes him furious. It makes him that much angrier that the orchestrated absence of support is most bitterly felt at a time when their popularity is increasing, after significant military successes, despite the encirclement that they have to endure from now on. Moreover, he recalls having noted down this thought recently in his notebook: "The legend is taking on fabulous proportions, we have become invincible." He still thinks so.

The arrest, at the end of last April, of the young French intellectual, Régis Debray, dispatched by Fidel Castro several months ago, was turned against the propaganda of the Barrientos regime. The caricature of a trial to which he had been subjected caused, in the end, the dictatorship to fall a bit more in world opinion.

Won over by the desire to conclude his narration, he continues: "The seventeen of us left under a waning moon, the march was very tiresome, and we left many traces in the canyon where we were. There are no houses nearby, but there are some potato fields irrigated from the same creek." He is worried that the fatigue could play tricks on them. All the men are weak, pale as wax, and cadaverous. They have to carry packs weighing thirty kilos. When they are thirsty, they sometimes drink their urine, and, when hungry, they devour rotting meat full of worms. He knows that some of them even have hallucinations because of lack of sleep. Above all, he knows that he himself verged on madness when, bewitched by exhaustion and anger, he killed his mule at the beginning of August. The psychological impact on the group had been terrible. For that reason, he wants to set an example more than ever. He decided not to explain it but, right before the break, he had to motivate the combatants again, by scaling a rock that blocked the path. The opening of 1.5 meters at the top of the rock had to be cleared in order to pass above a well of icy water and no one wanted to attempt it. Proof that morale is in low spirits. Sensing fatigue coming over him, he ends his daily account: "At 2:00 we stopped to rest, since it was useless to continue advancing. . .

"The army gave strange information about the presence of 250 men in Serrano to prevent the passage of those encircled, saying there were thirty-seven, and giving our refuge as being between the river Acero and the Oro. The news seems to be diversionary.

"Altitude: 2000 meters."

This is one of the highest points of their long march. He checks his altimeter and puts it in his pack, among all the books.

His books were the subject of recurrent jokes on the part of his companions. They said his backpack resembled a library more than an armory. That had never prevented him from taking care of his weapons. Further, he always kept an eye on his M4 rifle, as well as his revolver, and knew exactly where his Solingen dagger was to be found. He does not recall often having been unarmed. His father had taught him the basics of shooting when he was only five years old. Moreover, his father had made a point of slipping a revolver into his pocket, at the last minute, when he left for his first trip with Granado. As for the guerilla-doctor of the Sierra Maestra, he had not hesitated long when, on account of the weight of it all, he had to choose between the bullets and the medical kit: he was a revolutionary first. For him, weapons represented a political means necessary to carry out the struggle and liberate the people who, deprived of democratic governments, were also subjected to exploitation and discrimination. Faced with dictatorships, pacificism would not work—he knew that since Guatemala—and armed struggle could pay off—he knew that since Cuba. A handful of militants could have an effect on History. Before leaving for Cuba, there had been only a handful to train at a ranch in the city of Chalco, a few kilometers from Mexico City, under the command of General Alberto Bayo, a former Spanish Republican. After landing, there had still been only a handful of survivors. With the cry "Here, no one surrenders, *carajo*," shouted by his sorely missed comrade, Camilo Cienfuegos, they had continued to resist in a sugarcane plantation at Alegria del Pío. A handful tracked by seventeen thousand men. A handful, finally, when, on July 21, 1957, Fidel had made him *el comandante*, giving him a small golden star that he had gotten used to pinning to his beret. In many respects, the guerilla force still had the look of the Mexican army, counting many officers and few troops. For all that, and despite the hunger, disease, and fatigue, events had inexorably come together. Very quickly, the rear bases that he had known should be built, whether the one at El Hombrito or the one at La Mesa, had served as places for getting fresh supplies and also as places of dual-power, where one learned how to fight, but also to read. They had even established their own radio there, *Radio Rebelde*. Thirty years old, he had used up several months in protecting the Sierra against army incursions, organized by his sworn enemy, Sánchez Mosquera. The peasants themselves had consolidated this liberated zone, based on a new social organization, where literacy, health care, and justice were not only words. In fact, he had learned much from the people, in the countryside as in the cities. He had initially underestimated the role of the cities, after the failure of the first general strike. Then he was a participant in the meeting of the urban zones, at the end of 1958, when, at the head of the Ocho Column, he had begun to conquer the west of the island to liberate the cities of Las Villas and Santa Clara. The hardness of the living conditions, the march, and the combat, from the beginnings of the invasion up to the victory of Santa Clara on December 31, 1958, were branded on his body forever. This campaign was not just about military battles, with its successions of surrenders and shootings. It had brought about the revolution, in its wake, as it progressed. The agrarian reform moved forward to the rhythm of his column. Twenty-five months had led him to Havana, which he had discovered, on January 2, 1959, in a climate of general strike, celebration, and popular jubilation. These twenty-five months had transformed him.

His Cuban memories accompany him from the beginning of the Bolivian adventure. They comfort him, inspire him to advance, because they remind him that it is there, in the thick of the action, that he succeeds in surpassing himself and conducting himself as a new man, worthy of the new society that he wishes to build. The Cuban Revolution remains his compass, even if, from guerilla warfare to the ministries, it had, in the end, left him with the taste of being an unfinished experience. His course remained revolution across the world.

Between the meetings with Fidel at the beginning of 1959 in Havana and those on March 15, 1965, also in Havana, after three months of traveling in the course of which he had given his celebrated speech at Algiers, a page of history had turned. Upon his return, the discussion had lasted for two days. The friendship was always there, but the points of view diverged, notably on relations with Moscow. Not on Cuba. There had been, on his part, as much motivation to fight as to lead the revolution, in government as in all his functions. As ambassador, he was pleased to meet the great men of the planet: Nasser, Nehru, Tito, Sukarno, then Ben Bella, Khrushchev, Mao, and many others. He had put much work into agrarian reform, concerned to quicken the pace. In leading the Cuban National Bank, beginning in November 1959, he had taken great pleasure at defying the international markets by issuing bills with the signature "Che" and the effigy of Camilo Cienfuegos. As Minister of Industry, from February 1961, he had, even at the risk of underestimating Cuban realities, led a volunteer labor program to give Cuba a minimum of economic independence.

He had blossomed in his life as a Cuban. He was a credit to his double nationality, acquired since the triumph of the revolution, but which he had given up before starting off again. He had, of course, been indefatigable during the failed landing of the Americans and Cuban opposition at Playa Girón in the Bay of Pigs on April 17, 1961. He had been one of the main leaders. Yet, at the same time, he wanted above all, always and forever, to learn in every field, mainly in mathematics, thanks to regular courses. And he had continued to learn from the people directly. He valued their attitude, particularly during the voluntary workdays that he had instituted and in which he actively participated. In short, he had been proud to be Cuban.

He could not precisely pinpoint when the link with the Soviet authorities had begun to fray, before there was a total running battle going on. Perhaps it had been during the conduct of the missile crisis, the week of October 22 to October 28, 1962, when the world had held its breath, fearing a third world war between the two blocs. Khrushchev had then backed down in the face of Kennedy's ultimatum, removing the Soviet missiles from the island, without even warning Fidel. Perhaps it had been at the moment of the public debates on the topic of the transition to socialism, where he had not hesitated to stand up to the orthodox conceptions of the Soviet camp. In fact, at the National Bank as well as the Ministry of Industry, he had, to the greatest extent possible, acted to curb the profitability of the bank loans granted by the Big Brother in order to allow national industry to use to the highest degree possible the liquidities necessary for its operation. He did not understand that the loans granted by the Soviet countries to the third world countries could be, just like with capitalism, financially profitable. Maybe this rupture was produced during the period when, without wanting to, he had gradually appeared as one of the most ardent spokesmen for the poor countries, acting against imperialism on the international stage, in independence from, perhaps even in defiance of, the bureaucracies of the East. Whatever it may be, between his first triumphal welcome in Red Square in Moscow, November 7, 1960, and his last series of official trips around the world at the beginning of 1965, irremediable disputes had appeared.

The letter that he had left Fidel before "disappearing," which was made public in October 1965, was a letter of farewell. History continued, but part of his own history was behind him and took him away forever from his children—Hildita, Aleidita, Camilo, Celia, and Ernesto—to whom he had also addressed a posthumous letter.

The noise of his aluminum mess kit falling to the ground, thrown when his pack fell over, wakes him with a start. He was sleeping. He casts a quick glance at his watch: 4:00. It is time to leave. He looks at Benigno, who is sleeping deeply. He remembers again the moment when this young peasant, seventeen years old, had joined the ranks of the Cuban guerillas, after his pregnant wife had been murdered by the army. Benigno, who had been determinedly learning how to read and write since then, and who says not to keep a travel diary. But he only half-believes him and is not truly upset with him. He looks upon him fondly. Benigno symbolizes, at bottom, his own political epoch, the decade that passed between Cuba and Bolivia. He had written to his parents to reassure them during the military campaign with Fidel: "I have lost two lives, there are five remaining to me." Che had lost one life in the adventures of his youth, a second in the making of the Cuban Revolution, and another in extending the revolution in Latin America. He would be ready to wager that there are more lives remaining to him, still.

He shakes him tenderly: "Beni, we have to move out."

This October 8, 1967, the troop begins the march again. It is quickly encircled, denounced by a peasant who had seen them pass the preceding night near his potato field. Facing the fire of a hundred rangers with his men, *el comandante* is wounded in the right leg. He is arrested and held in the village of La Higuera. There, in a schoolroom, on October 9, at the beginning of the afternoon, Ernesto Guevara, called "Che" because of the typically Argentine interjection he pronounced at each sentence, is murdered with two shots fired by a soldier named Mario Terán. The latter acted on the orders of the Bolivian government, which had been working for weeks in close and open collaboration with the CIA.

Che leaves behind him his diary, his battles, and the legend of one who died for his ideas. Humanist adventurer for some, lay saint for others, a red Robin Hood for many, and revolutionary forever, Che embodies the hope that has remained intact in new generations to change the world by all means necessary.

1. A Marxist Humanism

There is a famous joke in Havana. During a meeting of the Cuban leadership, shortly after the revolution, Fidel asked the assembly: "Is there an economist in the hall?" Che raised his hand. He was immediately named president of the National Bank. At the end of the meeting, Fidel, taken aback, said to him: "I didn't know that you were an economist!" Che responded: "*Carajo*, I thought the question was: 'is there a communist in the hall?'" Humor aside, it is certain that Guevara publicly proclaimed his adherence to communist ideas, even before the Cuban Revolution.

Forty years after his death, it seems that Che has been spared the discredit which has crippled communist ideology at the beginning of the twenty-first century, in the wake of Stalinism and "real socialism." Thus, Che leaves to History the mark of one who denounced the indifference of Moscow to the national liberation struggles of people who sought to remove their countries from capitalist domination.

Che's subversive and romantic political epic was, during his time, a real inspiration for an international workers' movement locked within the confines of the Cold War. It is still today a breeding ground of ideas and an original source of stimulation. In fact, at a time in which capitalism has spread everywhere, Che's shadow still hangs over the heights of Chiapas in Mexico, among the Zapatista peasant rebels. It extends to Chávez's Venezuela. It floats above the processions of the alterglobalization movement, which contests the *diktat* of the predatory new world order over the economy, society, and the environment. Guevara is far more than a free communist, emancipated from the Soviet ideological yoke. Beyond the incidents with the Kremlin, Che knew how, through his own thinking, to give a new and lasting impulse to the universal project of social transformation, a project that he wished to see each person appropriate individually. For him, an understanding of socialism can only be realized at the personal level, closest to the intimate concerns of the exploited individual. If the revolution becomes impersonal, it breaks the palpable connection with human beings. By individualizing the political, Che hoped to cause the seed of emancipatory principles and processes to germinate in a maximum number of consciousnesses. The history of humanity is distinctive in that it is made by human beings.

Originally, Che's revolutionary humanism did not lead his action and ideas towards the renovation of Marxism. He was not seeking to give the latter a more human wrapping. His thinking was not constructed along such lines. Rather, his thinking pushed him towards Marxism because it is in this project that his initial humanist commitment found an objective in line with his own intellectual and political development. From his first adolescent trips in Latin America to his revolutionary combat in Cuba, the Congo, and Bolivia, his ideological matrix was never fixed. On the contrary, it was always in movement, under perpetual questioning, constant examination, prompted by a thirst for discovery. He did not find ready-made answers in selective readings of the "superficial and cardboard Marxism of the Russians," as Paco Ignacio Taibo II recalls in his biography *Guevara, Also Known as Che.*[1] The strongest commitment came from himself, his guts, his heart, and his head, a head eager to understand and know.

The period in which he developed was marked by colonialism, with its wars and racism, and by the decolonization movement, characterized by numerous wars of liberation against imperialism in Asia, Africa, and Latin America. Undoubtedly, the era was open to renewed political expectations after decades of sterile thought by the bureaucracy in Moscow. The time seemed ripe for new thinking and stimulated ideological emulation. By following his own path, Malcolm X in the United

States, who broke with the Black Muslims in 1964, arrived at conclusions similar to Che's on the eve of his assassination in February 1965: he came to advocate an open, humanist, and internationalist Marxism. Two lives. Two assassinations. Two journeys cut short by a death order from the uneasy upholders of the American order.

His political quest gradually led Che to the original Marxism, the one in which humanity and the individual were everything, the root and the goal of the egalitarian project. This is a global political project that forms a chain in which the human being, as principal actor and authentic revolutionary subject, becomes the common theme that links all the stages of the social transformation: from a revolt personally affected and provoked by the injustices of the current society to the blossoming of the individual encouraged by the new society. Che made a quotation from the Cuban poet and revolutionary José Martí his standard: "A real man should feel on his own cheek the blow given to another man's cheek."[2] To be on the edge of revolt, to be indignant, is to sense one's belonging to all of humanity, in a common destiny, and that is already to act. Humanity is situated at the same level as the family. Responding to someone named María Rosario Guevara, who asked him if it is possible that they have common ancestors, he responded: "I do not believe that we are descended from very close ancestors, but if you are capable of trembling with indignation each time that an injustice is committed in the world, then we are comrades, which is more important."[3] Che sought to validate a universal relation in which each of us would be led to interiorize our own well-being as a function of the well-being of our fellow human beings. This is not a question of an altruism resigned to endure the hardships of others as a burden, but, on the contrary, acting to change one's own lot, and the fate of others too, as a reciprocal achievement in mutual growth. He defended this idea in front of the young communists of Cuba: "every Young Communist must be essentially human and be so human that he draws closer to humanity's best qualities. . . . Developing to the utmost the sensitivity to feel anguished when a man is murdered in any corner of the world and to feel enthusiasm when a new banner of freedom is raised in any corner of the world."[4] To liberate humanity from its chains by fighting against individual alienation and defending ethical values—that is Che's original contribution to Marxism.

REVOLUTION FOR THE HUMAN BEING

His commitment to the revolution is explained first of all by his desire to liberate humanity from the invisible cage in which society encloses men and women when they are condemned to remain only wolves in relation to other men and women. Socialism (communism) has no meaning—and cannot triumph—if it does not represent a project for civilization, a social ethic, a model of a society totally antagonistic to the values of petty individualism, fierce egoism, competition, the war of all against all in the capitalist system. His approach to the revolution is above all a matter of human encounters. There was no lack of the latter during the first journey that he made across Latin America on a motorcycle with his friend, Alberto Granado. Together they discovered regions scarred by the voraciousness of the United Fruit Company, which had been pillaging wealth, lands, soil, and human lives for more than a half-century already. "All this wandering around 'Our America with a capital A' has changed me more than I thought," he wrote in opening his account *The Motorcycle Diaries: Notes on a Latin American Journey*.[5] With workers, peasants, miners, Indians, and others met by chance on the journey, he talked and exchanged opinions, which are as valuable as any evidence, and was aware of the solidarity to be established with those who suffer. Guevara, apprentice doctor, thus goes hand in hand with Guevara the revolutionary. Henceforth, he not only wanted to care for his fellow humans, but also to shield them from the cogwheels of the capitalist machine that devours and crushes people in order to spit them out again under the form of profits. "I discovered that it was impossible to cure sick children because of a lack of means, and I saw the deterioration produced by malnutrition and constant repression," he recalled in a speech on August 19, 1960, about these journeys. The road that led him to Marxism is inseparable from the faces encountered on that road, which form something like an animated backdrop. His course is a gradual political development that embraced the fate of all those he encountered. This course was accelerated during the military *coup d'état* in Guatemala in 1954, supported by the

United States, which ended the progressive reform program of the then current government. Che was a direct witness to the overthrow of President Jacobo Arbenz by a military junta. This experience only concentrated and epitomized all the tragic consequences of a counter-revolution that betrays the hopes of those who believe loyally in change: the omnipresence of U.S. economic and political power within Guatemalan ruling class circles, the violence of the wealthy classes in reaction to the social reforms underway, the ineffectiveness of the pacifism of Jacobo Arbenz, who had no idea how to oppose the revocation of the policy to which he had given the impetus, and the refusal of Guatemala's Stalinist communists to distribute arms to the people.

Che's Mexican exile, which followed this episode, offered him the opportunity to read a large number of Marxist-Leninist works and begin long discussions with militants, particularly with Castroite Cuban refugees, who had failed to take the Moncada Barracks. Their project to organize a landing on the island in order to liberate Cuba from the Batista dictatorship immediately found an echo in the turmoil of his new ideas.

Won over to Marxism before other Cuban leaders, Ernesto Guevara allowed the others to come to the conclusions to which he had come some time before, at their own pace and based on their own experiences. This is his idea of Marxism: an ideology that does not impose itself. In his eyes, adherence to this project can only be to what the project itself represents, that is, to something constantly changing. For him, a current of ideas whose essence rests on critical reflection can only make sense if each person adheres to it freely, through his or her own thinking. It was thus still as an Argentine and already a Marxist that Che intervened in the Cuban Revolution with one concern in mind: that the Cuban Revolution discover "by its own means the path that Marx pointed out."[6]

There is nothing dogmatic about Che's Marxism. No concept is established forever, and there are no ideas that cannot be thrown out. It was as a Marxist that he criticized Marx himself. For example, Che did not share the less than laudatory interpretation that Marx made of the actions of Simón Bolívar, important leader in the liberation of Latin America in the nineteenth century. First of all, he thought that Marx underestimated and denigrated the real inspiration that Bolívar provided in terms of hope and liberty for millions of oppressed people, defying colonialists and frontiers. Then Che, like all revolutionaries from the continent, placed his commitment in an historical relation to the battles of Bolívar in Venezuela and Colombia, Martí in Cuba, and Sandino in Nicaragua. These battles have distant roots, buried for centuries in the lands of Latin America, which resisted the assaults of the conquistadors of yesterday and still resists them today.

Worse still, according to him, Marx and Engels's point of view on the nationalities and races of Latin America peddled, in part, the ignorance, prejudices, and stereotypes of the political climate of the era—an analysis deemed "unacceptable in our days" by Che. However, what he considered to be errors of judgment does not alter, in his eyes, Marx's theoretical edifice, because revolutionaries do not necessarily have all the right answers on every subject. He even justifies a dose of prudence, not hesitating to offer surprising praise for improvisation, which encourages, according to him, learning in action: "Revolutions . . . are not always, or almost never or maybe never, mature and scientifically planned, they are made with passions, improvisations of people in their struggles for social demands, they are never perfect."[7]

Marxism is a guide for action. The operative principle of reality is "no construction will resemble any other." His anti-dogmatic Marxism, openly proclaimed from the beginning of the 1960s, clearly broke with the sectarian and narrow concepts dictated by the Soviet bureaucracy. For all that, Che's anti-dogmatism never diminished his fundamental and strong attachment to Marx's thought. His Marxism was not for convenience and his enthusiasm was complete. He made Marx's entire work his own: from the *Economic and Philosophical Manuscripts*, drafted by the young Marx in 1844, to *Capital*. With a critical eye, but faithful adherence, Che followed the main themes of his own humanist project in Marx's work. With the young Marx, the one who "thought about man's liberation and considered communism the solution to the contradictions that produced man's alienation,"[8] he felt great affinities. Far from being put off by the thick volumes of *Capital*, Guevara studied the relations of production examined in minute detail by the German philosopher, the relations that unite people with one another as social beings. He also found here evidence of priorities "with a humanist character in the best sense of the term."[9] Distinct from its bourgeois or religious variants, Guevara's humanism does not pretend to be able to deal with the emancipation of individuals by eluding the questions of oppression, exploitation, and the class struggle that continually shape society. For him, the advent of the truly human era can only be devised through a global and revolutionary settling of social inequalities.

THE HUMAN BEING FOR THE REVOLUTION

The human being, then, remains the profound reason for the revolution. But human beings are also the means, the support, and the actors of the revolution, at each of its phases, before, during, and after.

In this manner, Che unearthed an old Marxist idea, buried under the ideological detritus of the parties of the traditional Left. The idea that "the emancipation of the workers will be the work of the workers themselves." Both Social Democracy and the Stalinist Communist parties made a travesty of this simple idea. The former, gradually imprisoned in the established institutional apparatus, renounced changing society. The latter, guided by the superior interests of Moscow, feared revolutionary upsurges that, by their very nature, would upset the order of things and displease the wealthy classes and the *apparatchiks*. Guevara thus returned to the sources of Marxism and to its founding spirit: humanity can henceforth interpret and understand the course of the world, and it can also transform it. Revolutions are not the result of a magic operation or a mechanical process induced by History. They are not ordained. They are the result of the intervention of humanity in its own destiny, a conscious intervention, both individual and collective. People are not the pawns of superior forces that are somehow beyond them, forces which set the exploited class against the exploiters in struggle against one another. People are, on the contrary, "living expressions"[10] because it is they who make History. The transition from one type of society into another can only be the work of human hands; it does not fall from the sky. By no longer granting to "human liberation" the significance of "a conscious act" and by underestimating, even denying humanity the "role of conscious actor of history," the parties of the traditional Left ultimately lost sight of the fact that "without the consciousness, which encompasses [one's] awareness as a social being, there can be no communism."[11]

Unwittingly acknowledging the abandonment of their supposed principles, these same parties often reproached Che with having been too voluntarist in his activism, even "leftist,"[12] by favoring the initiatives of a minority over the struggles of the majority of the whole population. For these critics, this voluntarism is epitomized by Che's statement: "The duty of a revolutionary is to make the revolution!" José Martí, however, said, well before Che, "the best means of telling is doing!" This Guevarist statement of the obvious is a stinging reproach to an often wait-and-see international Left that is passive, sometimes complicit with the capitalist system, and always bogged down in its institutional, diplomatic, and electoral relations. Che thought, in fact, that the activities of a minority can serve as a catalyst, but only from the moment that that minority succeeds in achieving a broader unity. The avowed aim consists of giving "the masses consciousness of their destiny and the certainty that it is possible."[13]

To shape consciousnesses, to provoke the thinking and commitment of the greatest number—that is Guevara's prime political objective. For that, he calls to each individual. For him, the people are not an informal mass, but "a multidimensional entity [that] is not, as is sometimes pretended, the sum of the elements of one category (reduced to the same uniformity by the system imposed) acting as a docile herd."[14] The people are "a conscious aggregate of individuals who struggle for the same cause." The individual "actor in this strange and passionate drama that is the building of socialism" must be understood "in his twofold existence as a unique being and as a member of the community."[15] The individual is the "fundamental factor" of "the process when there existed only the seeds of socialism," and the individual must remain that factor over the course of the revolution itself, "specific, with first and last name."[16]

Ernesto Guevara establishes a complementary relation between the collective and the individual, between the global and the particular, within the revolutionary process. He recommends becoming "used to thinking collectively" and "at the same time, in everything we do as individuals, we should always be making sure our actions will not tarnish our own name or the name of the association to which we belong."[17] He encourages the "personality" of each to play a "role" in "mobilization and leadership."[18]

Guevara thus refutes any project that comes down to formatting and normalizing humanity. He detects in that approach a failing incompatible with his idea of communism. Each person should retain a critical attitude towards the course of things in the transition from one society to another, especially since people are often just feeling their way along in that context. From this point of view, Che did not hesitate to rebel: in October 1962, he publicly reproached the leadership of the Cuban Union of Young Communists with being "too docile, too respectful."[19] He encouraged them, rather, to declare "war on formalism of all types."[20]

In fact, Che places the personality of each person at the heart of the project of social transformation, before and during social upheavals, as they move from revolutionary turmoil to the revolution itself. After the revolution has triumphed in a single country, it can experience a second wind only by making new allies in the world for its cause, and it must make such allies in order to succeed in reaching its ultimate goal, i.e., its lasting consolidation. Thus, it is necessary to extend the revolution to the international scale. Che brings revolutionary internationalism back to personal feelings. Through a "love for humanity," in the name of a "brotherhood that surpasses distances and differences," he encourages youth not to be "limited by national borders" and to spread the revolution as an "uninterrupted task."[21] With regard to the American war against Vietnam, he urges each to "be overcome by anguish at this illogical fix in which humanity finds itself" represented by "the lonely situation of the Vietnamese people."[22] Guevara invites each person individually to influence the cycle of the revolution, from its beginnings to its planetary extension.

THE HUMAN BEING THROUGH THE REVOLUTION

The relation between the individual and the collective is, in Che's eyes, a complementary and dialectical relation. The individual is as valuable for the revolution as the latter is for the personality of each person. The society that Che hopes and prays for is, moreover, the "society of the communist man."[23] And, "to construct communism simultaneously with the material base of our society, we must create a new man."[24] To create "the new man" does not mean that Guevara has, *a priori*, an angelic assessment of human nature or that he entertains, even from a distance, the desire to clone a perfect humanity. Che does not support the standardization of the human species, from no matter where it originates. It is a question, in fact, of helping people to liberate themselves from all obstacles in order to be able to develop their own creativity and originality. In the same time period, Frantz Fanon, West Indian psychiatrist and militant of Algerian independence in the National Liberation Front (FLN), insisted also on the necessity of "setting people loose." These two both apprehended the human person in her full complexity, with negative and positive sides, and sought to build a society where the best could prevail over the worst on the basis of a human species that is capable of both the best and the worst. Rather than give an optimistic or pessimistic judgment on the human species, both prefer not to idealize really existing personalities, precisely in order to maintain the possibility of causing a new human ideal to emerge, to make a bet on the best on the basis of the real: "It is essential to use all the opportunities available to develop [individuals] to the fullest—educating [them] and obtaining from [them] the greatest benefit for the nation."[25]

Fanon, as much as Guevara, seeks to channel the redemptive energy that is likely to liberate each oppressed and exploited individual, by relying on the whole range of human feelings and resentments, from love to hate. Che proposes to surpass the contradictions found in this range of feeling: "It is necessary to become hardened without abandoning one's tenderness." Such a surpassing is difficult and Che knows from his own experience just how difficult it can be. In a letter addressed to his parents after his departure for Cuba, he recognizes that he is "extremely rigid in his acts" and that he "does not know how to express his tenderness" although he "has loved them very much." Perhaps it is for that reason that he insists so much on the necessary quality of human feelings: "Let me say, with the risk of appearing ridiculous, that the true revolutionary is guided by strong feelings of love. It is impossible to think of an authentic revolutionary without this quality."[26] Nevertheless, that does not prevent him from citing "hatred as an element of struggle, relentless hatred of the enemy that impels us over and beyond the natural limitations of man and transforms us into effective, violent, selective, and cold killing machines." He even adds: "Our soldiers must be thus; a people without hatred cannot vanquish a brutal enemy."[27] From a distance, such a statement can send chills down the spine. Fortunately, Che's actual behavior is far from this coldness, as can be witnessed in this passage from his Bolivian diary: "We took two more spies as prisoners: a lieutenant of the carabineers and a carabineer. They were given a lecture and set free."[28] In another extract from this moving document, Guevara tells how, perched on a hill overlooking the road, he took pity on two soldiers in a passing truck. They were cold, huddled in their blankets: "I didn't have the courage to fire on them. . . ."[29]

Che's era was marked by the violence of numerous dictatorships, with its share of tortures, executions, and disappearances. This raises the question of violence as a political subject in its own right for each popular resistance movement: is it necessary to use violence, should it only be in reaction to the existing brutality? Frantz Fanon, in his work *The Wretched of the Earth*, published in 1961, proposes to turn the colonizer's violence against itself: "The practice of violence binds them together as a whole, since each individual forms a violent link in the great chain, a part of the great organism of violence which has surged upward in reaction to the settler's violence in the beginning." He continues: "At the level of individuals, violence is a cleansing force. It frees the native from his inferiority complex and from his despair and inaction; it makes him fearless and restores his self-respect."[30]

Fanon, like Guevara, proposes to check human ambiguities by channeling them into a political approach that directs the violence internalized by all those who are subjected to oppression against the chains that imprison them. The problem is posed differently in a twenty-first century where a number of military dictatorships have given way to dictatorships of money. However, a relevant lesson remains: human ambivalence is not a problem, provided that humanity is turned towards emancipatory prospects. Che's position, at this level, whether he knows it or not, overlaps in part with the libertarian and anarchist approach of the Parisian Communarde Louise Michel, who, at the end of the nineteenth century, asserted: "I am not deserving . . . no more than I am a monster. We are all products of our era, that's all there is to it. Each of us has good and bad characteristics; that is common to everyone; but it does not matter what we are, if our work is great and covers us with its light, it is not a question of us in what we begin, it is a question of what will be for humanity when we are gone."[31]

The point is to change human beings in order to change society and vice versa. Thus, individual consciousness finds its rightful place in the revolutionary project. It should not act as a pretext for a Left that is resigned to change society on the basis of the idea that "it is necessary to change minds before changing society." Nor can the slate be wiped clean by a centralizing, grotesque, and narrow collectivism, which pretends that only changes in economic structure will change minds. Socialism is not only an economic change. It is also a profound moral and cultural revolution, breaking with the egoistical and venal utilitarianism of capitalist civilization. Revolutionary consciousness can only develop on the basis of values such as solidarity and equality.

A fascinating document on the evolution of Che Guevara's ideas is the transcript of the periodic discussions that he had with his collaborators in the Ministry of Industry. Large extracts from these appear in the same volume as the *Critical Notes on Political Economy*.[32] During a discussion in December 1963, the comrade minister explains: "Communism is a phenomenon of consciousness and not only a phenomenon of production; one cannot arrive at communism by the simple mechanical accumulation of a quantity of products placed at the disposal of the people. One can arrive at what Marx defines as communism . . . only if the human being is conscious." In fact, the construction of socialism is inseparable from certain ethical values, contrary to what the economistic doctrines of Stalin proclaim, which were taken up by Khrushchev and his successors. In an interview with the journalist Jean Daniel in July 1963, Guevara also indicates, in what was already an implicit critique of "real socialism": "Economic socialism without communist morality does not interest me. We are fighting against poverty but at the same time against alienation. . . . If communism ignores facts of consciousness, it can be a method of distribution, but it is no longer a revolutionary morality."

If socialism aspires to fight against capitalism and defeat it on its terrain, the terrain of productivism and consumerism, by using its means—the commodity form, competition, egoistical individualism—it is condemned to defeat. It cannot be said that Guevara foresaw the end of the USSR, but he had the intuition that a "socialist" system that does not tolerate divergences, that does not represent new values, that attempts to imitate its adversary, that has no other ambition than to reach and surpass the production of the capitalist centers, has no future.

For Che, socialism is the historical project of a new society, founded on values of equality, solidarity, collectivism, revolutionary altruism, free discussion, and popular participation. His increasing criticisms of "real socialism" as well as his practice as a leader and his reflection on the Cuban experience inspired this communist utopia, in the sense that Ernst Bloch gives to the word "utopia," a "landscape of desire."

The new society is under constant construction. Revolutions move forward at the same time as the possibility increases for each individual to leave behind the vestiges of the old world that necessarily subsist in consciousness, such as egoism, greed, racism, and sexism. To succeed in that aim, Che proposes to make society into a "gigantic school." The key to transformation lies in education, instruction, apprenticeship of the critical spirit, in the acquisition of knowledge and know-how, which Malcolm X compares to weapons. The solution is also found in culture, creation, efflorescence of the arts, daily activities, and even in work, which has thus become "man's greatest dignity . . . a pleasure given to man."[33] The enthusiasm with which Che imagines potential, unexplored capacities left fallow in each individual recalls Louise Michel again: "The future human being will have new senses! One detects them breaking through in the being of our era."[34]

For Guevara, the new human being is first of all, out of concern for setting an example, a conscious revolutionary who must be irreproachable and the best. She must be the mirror in which those who have not yet acquired revolutionary ideas recognize themselves, the person who fights and acts on the basis of a revolutionary morality and ethical values founded on dignity and respect for human life. "Revolutionary conduct is the reflection of revolutionary faith, and when someone claims to be revolutionary and does not act like a revolutionary that person is nothing more than a clown."[35] His revolutionary morality, which views humanity as the supreme value, dictates a true code of ethical conduct. Once again, consciously or not, Che has placed himself within an underground current of international socialism. Auguste Blanqui, great revolutionary figure of nineteenth-century France, although completely secular and rejecting the religious approach, evoked a "revolutionary faith" capable of inciting "enthusiasm for liberty [within] people who then no longer obey vile monetary interests, but the most noble passions of the spirit, the inspiration of a higher morality."[36] Rosa Luxemburg, German revolutionary socialist of the early twentieth century, gave revolutionary morality an important place in the struggle and debate of ideas. José Carlos Mariátegui, founder of Latin American Marxism at the beginning of the twentieth century, did not envisage revolutionary commitment without a romantic spirit, without the fieriness of a passionate and heroic will, or without adhering to a revolutionary mysticism. In his posthumous work, *Defensa del marxismo*, republished in Cuba in the first issue of the review *Tricontinental*, he devotes several pages to the "ethical function of socialism." He concludes with this affirmation: socialist ethics "do not arise mechanically from economic interest, they are affirmed in the class struggle, practiced with an heroic spirit, a passionate will."

Was Che inspired by these lines, by this socialist tradition marked by romanticism? That is difficult to say. But by giving ethical significance to the socialism that he wishes to construct, he radically breaks with the orthodox and icy version of "real socialism" found in the countries of the East. At the same time, his ethical conception remains, posthumously, the best response to all those detractors who seek, many years later, to make him into a bloodthirsty person. Yes, Che killed during the guerilla war and during the revolution. He led an armed struggle, with the rank of comandante, to overthrow the Batista dictatorship. Yes, rather than hide behind subalterns, he himself directed the executions of several dozen torturers and leaders of the Batista regime in the first hours of the revolution. One can regret this revolutionary justice, but nothing permits comparing it to the Stalinist political purges. Each liberation movement encounters this dilemma. The liberation of France in 1944 and 1945 ended in the execution of thousands of collaborators. The Sandinistas of Nicaragua preferred to grant amnesty to the henchmen of the Somoza dictatorship. Their exemplary generosity was not paid back in kind: a number of former members of the Somoza National Guard, upon being freed, joined the ranks of the Contras, a counterrevolutionary force armed by the United States, which increased killings among the civilian population.

All accounts of the era, from both sides, agree on the fact that Che always had the greatest respect for life, opposing summary executions and pointless combat. Guevara also explicitly condemned terrorism: "Assaults and terrorism in indiscriminate form should not be employed."[37] He regularly pleaded with his companions to prevent gratuitous killings: "We are not like them." He gave medical treatment to prisoners and gave strict orders to institute "the widest possible clemency": "It is a good policy, so long as there are no considerable bases of operations and invulnerable places, to take no prisoners. Survivors ought to be set free. The wounded should be cared for with all possible resources at the time of the action."[38] Che publicly regretted the extreme character of the death penalty. Moreover, he did not participate in military tribunals. To organize executions legally with courts was, in his eyes, the best way to avoid mass slaughters. It is one thing, with the distance that separates us from the events, to regret Che's philosophical approbation for the use of capital punishment, even if this was probably done reluctantly. For our part, we reject it in principle. But it is another thing to pass off Guevara as an executioner and murderer. His detractors would have difficulty creating a police record for him.

For all that, not to recognize the limits of Che's actions would, for those who still claim to adhere to his ideas, amount to amputating Guevarist thought from its spinal column: the critical spirit. His faults are certainly nestled within the recesses of his positive qualities. It is, for example, well known that Che made the highest demands on his own behavior. He refused, to excess, anything that could more or less appear as favorable treatment, be it remuneration, food, housing, or medical care. He set the highest expectations for himself concerning exemplary behavior in relation to others. The revolutionary morality that he followed in a disciplined and rigorous manner could sometimes be draped in a hyper-selective, vanguardist discourse, verging on elitism. In his *Bolivian Diary*, for example, Che states: ". . . this type of struggle gives us the opportunity not only to turn ourselves into revolutionaries, the highest level of the human species, but it also allows us to graduate as men; those who cannot reach either one of these two stages should say so and leave the struggle."[39] The extreme conditions of guerilla warfare obviously explain the merciless character of such words. However, the boundary seems rather flimsy here between the political project and military obligations. Where does the new man stop and the superman begin? This ambiguity, moreover, leaves little room for the "new woman." However conscious of the "manifestations of discrimination" against women, even within the revolutionary party, and convinced of the necessity for the "total" and "internal" liberation of women, Che still felt the "weight of tradition."[40] There is also a shadowy political area that arises from the tricky issue of the democratic organization of guerilla movements. The context of war obviously prohibits systematic deliberations in regular assemblies that would control all the decisions of military leadership from A to Z. The balance between effectiveness and democracy within an armed struggle remains a current concern. The search for this equilibrium is epitomized well enough by the slogan of the Zapatista Army of National Liberation (EZLN—*Ejército Zapatista de Liberación Nacional*), which rose up on January 1, 1994, in Chiapas: "Lead by obeying."

In the same way, the sacrificial concept that Che has of the militant commitment to work, within the family or in combat, gives rise to a legitimate debate. Certainly, this approach should only be understood in the precise situation of the events in which Guevara was acting: a conflict initiated by a handful of men chased by several thousand soldiers of the Batista dictatorship, then the struggle undertaken by a small island, Cuba, against its worst enemy, the United States, situated a few dozen kilometers from its coast. In opposition to any suicidal concept, he gives this sacrificial commitment a sense of life, of survival even, by pushing each individual to dig deep down inside herself to find a new energy so as to increase her personal possibilities tenfold. But placed in a situation of extreme crisis, the idea of sacrifice can take turns that are difficult to control. During the missile crisis in October 1962, for example, the people of the world held their breath during the long hours of the ultimatum Kennedy gave to Khrushchev to remove the Soviet missiles secretly based in Cuba. A few months later, Che said these words: "Here is the electrifying example of a people prepared to suffer atomic immolation so that its ashes may serve as the foundation for new societies. And when an agreement was reached by which the atomic missiles were removed, without asking our people, we were not relieved or thankful for the truce. . . ."[41] First of all, it is clear that Che, who usually recommended "the avoidance of any pointless sacrifice," was exaggerating: he mainly sought to denounce the Soviet betrayal of Cuban confidence. In fact, the Soviets made all their decisions during the crisis behind the back of the revolutionary government of Cuba. Nothing, however, justifies the hypothesis of the collective sacrifice of a people nor the use of nuclear weapons, a barbarism *par excellence*. After Hiroshima and Nagasaki, the young Che understood that nuclear weapons take no care to distinguish between the oppressed and their oppressors.

Che's thought has limits. It is, in part, incomplete and tentative. However, stimulated by the urgency of the times in which he lived, his political thought, directed at a humanist revolutionary objective, restores individuality to a central place in the socialist project. It does not leave the necessity of understanding the individual to capitalism, which deals only with the satisfaction of personal ambitions in an egoistical fashion. Capitalist society creates individual aspirations for the greatest number without ever making it possible to satisfy them. This contradiction between capital and the individual is overcome only at the price of an alienation that Che denounces: "The alienated man has an invisible umbilical cord which ties him to the whole society: the law of value. It acts on all facets of his life, shaping his road and destiny."[42] Against the egoism of a society governed by the law of the jungle, "where one can only arrive by means of the failure of others,"[43] Che envisages the flourishing of the "future man" through the "close dialectical unity that exists between the individual and the mass. . . ."[44] The emancipation of the individual is carried out all the more as the work is collective and done in solidarity. At this moment, the new man "achieve[s] total awareness of his social being, which is equivalent to his full realization as a human creature. . . . In order for it to attain the characteristic of being free, work must acquire a new condition; man as a commodity ceases to exist. . . ."[45] "Man begins to liberate his thought from the bothersome fact that presupposes the need to satisfy his animal needs through work. He begins to see himself portrayed in his work and to understand its human magnitude. . . ."[46] In the celebrated text *Socialism and Man in Cuba*, Che claims more wealth for each individual, wealth that is not counted in "wages," the quantity "of imported pretty things," or "in kilograms of meat" consumed.[47] He is speaking of human wealth, a perspective often neglected by the revolutionary movement over the course of the twentieth century, outside of certain libertarian currents. Guevara thus disputes the notion of individuality found in capitalist society, which claims to have made the individual its standard and its trademark. But the freedom granted by capitalists in this area is also only an illusion, an illusion fought by Marxism for a long time on the terrain of individualism itself, before Soviet manuals eliminated the latter. Antonio Gramsci, the important Italian Marxist, did not criticize individualism in itself, but reproached it with having become "anti-historical" under capitalism, "manifested in the individual appropriation of wealth. . . ." Arguing with the Catholic thought of the time, he added: "if it has become impossible for all to have possessions, why should it be anti-spiritual to look for a form of property in which material forces complete and contribute to the constitution of all personalities?" Moreover, "human 'nature' [resides] not within the individual but in the unity of man and material forces."[48] These are visionary words that, a half-century later, acquire a new force when considered in the light of Guevara's humanist contribution.

2. *Socialist Revolution or Caricature of Revolution?*

Che is not a moralistic dreamer, a utopian divorced from reality. His human and fraternal idea of an authentic communist society is accompanied by a lucid, concrete, and realistic analysis of the socioeconomic, political, and military situation of Latin America, as well as the other continents exploited by imperialism.

Guevara's pragmatism, however, does not reflect the realism of the contemporary period, very fashionable in the political class, which, above all, serves as a pretext for maintaining the current the social order. His pragmatism does not consist of adapting to existing reality but rather of understanding it for the purpose of radically changing it. Che does not oppose morality to politics. His pragmatism does not contradict a certain type of utopia, so long as that utopia consists of continuously maintaining the open-eyed imagination necessary for the construction of a new society. Guevara has a head full of dreams, but that head is firmly screwed onto his shoulders. His relation to power, an existential problem for revolutionaries, proves it. He participated in the government of Cuba, beginning in 1959, without ever denying his instinctive mistrust towards the institutional system. He also knew how to leave it and undertake his political battles by other means. Politics grows quickly at ground level, in contact with the popular masses, and often dies in ministry corridors.

Today, cynicism in politics seems to be triumphant. Some parties of the workers' movement have learned to manage the business of capitalism loyally, alternating in power. According to them, the Left is henceforth divided into two camps: those who accept participating in power and those who refuse to do so on principle, those who get their hands dirty and those who are condemned to political impotence and futile opposition. Forty years after his murder in 1967, Che's experience remains a hopeful example, countering theories used too often to justify the Left's repudiations of power. In fact, his experience proves that both independence from power and action within a government, in his case the revolutionary Cuban government, are not incompatible. Thus, it is possible to return to the true nature of the cleavage that has long divided the Left concerning the exercise of power: on the one hand, those who still want to change society and, on the other, those who mold themselves to the existing system. For Che, the abstract question of whether or not to participate in government misses the mark. The real question is: participate in order to do what, on what basis, to build what type of power and, above all, what society? To lose one's soul at the head of a state that remains in the hands of the oppressors or to cause that state to fall in order to construct a socialist power by and for the people?

The history of Che's political life is still, in the present, an effective remedy to cure the dullness, resignation, and fatalism that pollute the current climate. It was a short and hurried political life, barely fifteen years, of which ten were devoted to armed struggle for the revolution and five passed in the leadership of the Cuban revolutionary government as a minister. By participating in power without clinging to it, Che represents an exceptional case in the revolutionary movements of the twentieth century. His course synthesizes the key strategic problem that has beset the workers' movement since its origins: is it necessary to take power and, if so, how not to be taken in by it?

Guevara's approach avoids two pitfalls. First of all, it rejects all collusion with the state led by the dominant classes, which ineluctably leads to being encysted, then digested, by a state that remains that of the old society. Che is not delicate on the subject: "And in order to get permission to play this dangerous game one must show that one is a good boy, that one is not dangerous, that one would never think of assaulting army garrisons or trains, or destroying bridges, or bringing revolutionary justice to hired thugs of the reaction or to torturers, or going to the mountains. One cannot state resolutely the only and violent affirmation of Latin America: the final struggle for her redemption."[1] He thus sets the cat among the pigeons, tarnishing the reputation of both social-democratic parties and numerous Stalinist communist parties bogged down in national union governments.

For all that, Guevara does not share the libertarian point of view, or more precisely the anarchist one, which rejects any form of centralized government. Che does not think that the exploited can change society without taking power away from the hands of those who exploit them. "To conquer something, we have to take it away from someone else. . . . We have to conquer our national sovereignty, and we have to take it away from foreign monopolies,"[2] he explains. Che adds: "The people cannot even dream about sovereignty if there is no power that responds to the people's interests and aspirations. Popular power does not mean merely that the people control the council of ministers, the police, the courts of law, and all the governmental machinery, but it also means that the economic institutions are beginning to be controlled by the people. Revolutionary power or political sovereignty is the instrument to conquer economic independence and to make a reality of national sovereignty."[3]

TAKING POWER

It is primarily in reaction to the ineffectiveness of reformism that Che came to such conclusions. The reformist strategy claims to be able to apply measures in small strokes, in a slow and gradual manner, without *a priori* disrupting the social order. Che discovered, from the tragic results of the Guatemalan *coup d'état* that overthrew the government of Jacobo Arbenz in 1954, that this approach, even when it is sincere, is doomed to failure. It does not prepare the people to protect its liberation from the violent reaction of the minority that appropriated the wealth produced by the labor of the majority and now feels threatened. It leaves economic power in the same hands, those whose privilege fears, like the plague, the least reform if it is at all daring. This is the case with agrarian reform, which consists of taking back the land from the wealthiest and redistributing it to those who work it. In favor of this type of reform, Che concludes that it is illusory to think of imposing it without a comprehensive and revolutionary change in all of society, from economic structures to government ones. In Guatemala, he takes note of the failure of reformism and swings over to the revolutionary camp. Summarizing his own course, Che says: "I was born in Argentina, I fought in Cuba, and I began to be a revolutionary in Guatemala."[4] Che understood immediately that the 1954 events were only one episode among many others, one of those pages that riddles the History of humanity fighting for its rights. A senseless repetition of the past, a shadow of the Paris Commune of 1871, which sinisterly prefigured the dark moments that were still to come in the sad fate of Latin America, particularly Chile in 1973. The same demons for the same conclusions: without defense, when the people loyally rise up to reclaim more wealth and power, they always end up by being repressed and massacred, be this at the *Mur des Fédérés* (Communards' Wall) at the Père Lachaise cemetery in Paris, under a volley of shots from the *Versaillais*,[5] or in the stadium in Santiago by Pinochet's militias.

Those who present Guevara as a *desperado*, aspiring only to die with weapons in hand, retain only the image of the man in the military beret, forgetting what is bubbling underneath: his revolutionary ideas. Armed struggle is a means and was the best instrument for achieving the transformation of society *in the precise political conditions of Latin America at that time*. Armed struggle is not necessarily the cornerstone of revolutionary combat. On the contrary, Che believes that it is only necessary to take up arms as a last resort, once all other solutions have been exhausted. In his eyes, the portion of violence or nonviolence in a revolution does not depend on the revolutionaries. It is proportional to the degree of resistance presented by the reactionary forces opposed to the birth of a new society. For Che, revolutionaries do not inevitably enter into conflict, becoming fanatical about the trigger. Moreover, he does not define peaceful transition as merely "the achievement of formal power by elections or through public opinion movements without direct combat," but rather as "the establishment of socialist power, with all of its attributes, without the use of armed struggle." For him, "it is reasonable then, that all the progressive forces do not have to initiate the road of armed revolution but must use—until the very last moment—every possibility of legal struggle within the bourgeois conditions."[6] In his *Guerilla Warfare*, Che pushes this analysis even further: "Where a government has come into power through some form of popular vote, fraudulent or not, and maintains at least an appearance of constitutional legality, the guerilla outbreak cannot be promoted, since the possibilities of peaceful struggle have not yet been exhausted."[7] He even imagines, "in special situations of crisis," that "peaceful struggle can be undertaken by mass movements" for the purpose of "obliging governments to cede power" and allowing "popular forces to take up power." Revolutionaries must above all determine the methods of their struggle as a function of the specific conditions with which they are confronted. The conditions in Latin America, a continent in the grip of brutal dictatorial regimes directly supported by the United States, provide little margin for maneuver in public and legal struggle. "We emphatically answer that, in the great majority of cases, this is not possible."[8] At best, revolutionaries only achieve formal power, without authority in the economic domain. As a result, he concludes from this particular set of circumstances: "Although one should not exclude the possibility of change beginning through the electoral process, the conditions that prevail in all [Latin American] countries make that possibility very remote." Haunted by the Guatemalan experience, the powerlessness followed by the total surrender of the Arbenz government, he wonders about the chances of success of a "legalist" strategy: "When we speak of winning power via the electoral process, our question is always the same: If a popular movement takes over the government of a country by winning a wide popular vote and resolves as a consequence to initiate the great social transformations which make up the triumphant program, would it not come into conflict right away with the reactionary classes of that country? Has the army not always been the repressive instrument of that class? If this is so, it is logical to suppose that this army will side with its class and enter the conflict against the new constituted government. By means of a *coup d'état*, more or less bloodless, this government can be overthrown and the old game renewed again, which will seem never to end."[9] Recall the fate of Salvador Allende in Santiago, Chile, September 11, 1973.

The political path that Guevara opens in Latin America breaks with the cowardly pacifism of a part of the Latin American Left, but is also in firm opposition to adventurism and militarism, because it is not a question of making war just to make war. In his article, "Guerilla Warfare: A Method" Guevara summarizes his frame of mind by citing Martí: "He who wages war in a country, when he can avoid it, is a criminal, just as he who fails to promote war which cannot be avoided is a criminal."[10]

In Che's eyes, guerilla warfare had become unavoidable in most countries of the continent. Thus, it is important to prepare for it actively and extend it to all of these countries, which he compares to a "volcano" whose rumblings could announce new revolutionary eruptions if effective catalysts were to create them.

For Che, this catalyst is guerilla warfare. It is a question of organizing several centers of armed struggle, above all in rural and mountainous areas, sparked by groups of guerillas. Che was inspired by the armed struggles in America, in the nineteenth century and the beginning of the twentieth century, led by Bolívar, Sandino, and even Zapata. He was aware of the methods of the Spanish Civil War in 1936. His ideas were in line with those of the new guerilla organizations that arose in the midst of the Second World War, the partisans in Europe and the anti-colonialists in Algeria, Africa, and Asia.

First of all, he counts on a rural guerilla war. He believes that it is in the countryside that the majority, who live in the poverty of the peasant condition, in which an explosive revolt lies dormant, is ready to burst out under the weight of centuries-long oppression and exploitation. It is in the gradually liberated zones that an agrarian reform should be applied as a priority under the control of the initial revolutionary structures. In revolutionary war, guerilla warfare makes it possible to gain this type of political, military, economic, and cultural position. Such bases of operation are necessary in order to win the war in its entirety, principally in the cities. From these guerilla centers, these *focos*, Che believes that the comprehensive struggle can be focused outward and win over the support of popular forces. Alternative powers appear against the central power and make the duality of power that is emerging between the new society that is being born and the old, condemned to disappear, more visible. Many criticisms have been made of Che's emphasis on guerilla warfare and his concept of the "*foco*." Some are well founded, others less so.

It is undoubtedly true that Che underestimates the political role of cities while overvaluing the political place of the peasantry. He does not denigrate workers' struggles, far from it. Nevertheless, his whole political plan of action rests, in terms of energy and political concerns, on small groups of guerillas. There is often a high price to pay, beyond being hounded by military forces, when organizing such groups in rather remote rural areas. The cost of giving priority to such a rural presence sometimes comes down to being divorced from militant networks in the cities, however essential. The working class in the cities is certainly a minority in numbers, but quite strong. It is also combative and essential for overturning capitalism. Without its involvement in the struggle, the outcome is almost decided in advance. For example, the idea that the Andes can become the Sierra Maestra of all of Latin America is not absurd in itself. But this rests on the condition of not neglecting the realities of each country, which have varying degrees of urbanization, and not overlooking the importance of the organizing activity that must be carried out with the exploited masses in the mines, cities, and companies.

Che viewed guerilla warfare as only the beginning of a necessary mass movement. In his article, "Guerilla Warfare: A Method," he is unequivocal: ". . . those who want to undertake guerilla warfare are criticized for forgetting mass struggle, implying that guerilla warfare and mass struggle are opposed to each other. We reject this implication for guerilla warfare is a people's war; to attempt to carry out this type of war without the population's support is the prelude to inevitable disaster. The guerilla is the combat vanguard of the people . . . supported by the peasant and worker masses of the region and of the whole territory in which it acts. Without these prerequisites, guerilla warfare is not possible."[11] To present Che as a loner, essentially on his own, and armed for the assault on the powerful is not dishonorable, but that is a purely hypothetical view. Che views guerilla warfare as a means to trigger a broad movement of the majority.

In this perspective, he also recognizes the centrality of the working class. As a Marxist, he knows that, given its key place in production, even when it is a minority, the working class can block the operation of the system at any moment. As a result, he pays close attention to the construction of an urban mass movement. The disagreements he had with the urban cadres of the July 26th Movement, the so-called "network of the plain," during the Cuban revolution, testify to the interest that he has in mobilizations in the city. While he reproaches them for underestimating the role of rural guerilla operations, he criticizes them, above all, for their lack of preparation and organization and their sectarian practices. Che knows that the faults of the revolutionary movement in the city are all the more unacceptable, since the repression would be terrible if the attempts at a general strike fail. That is, indeed, the sad result of the two aborted strikes in Cuba under Batista: the first spontaneous one in August 1957 and that of April 9, 1958, responding to the last-minute appeal of the revolutionary radio networks. On the other hand, the success of the insurrectionary general strike of January 1, 1959, dealt a deathblow to the dictatorship that no military victory could have replaced. Che knows this and is, at this level, part of the old tradition of the workers' movement that grants the insurrectionary general strike a crucial strategic significance in the people's taking power: "a most important factor in civil war."[12] Seizing power then is, for Che, a necessary step that should not be understood as the result of a violent revolutionary strike but rather as the result of a wide revolutionary movement of the majority, provoked in the rural areas, and in the cities as well, by the armed action undertaken by the guerillas. This is what happened in Cuba. In Bolivia, on the other hand, a narrower and more military view of the struggle seems to have predominated in his endeavor.

NOT TO BE TAKEN BY POWER

Che participated in seizing power and in its exercise, as head of the Department of Industries of the National Institute of Agrarian Reform, as President of the National Bank and as Minister of Industry from 1959 to 1964. He was a member of the revolutionary government, with no reluctance. He put a lot of effort into decisions, going into the field to observe the consequences of measures taken. He took part in the public debates about which choices to make in financial, economic, political, and industrial matters. But his involvement never made him drunk with power.

Che proved to be extremely disciplined with himself and refused anything that could appear as a convenience or privilege linked to the position that he occupied. He even required of himself, and his friends and relatives, voluntary working days, notably in the sugarcane fields, in order to participate in collective tasks, just like the nameless mass of people. Because Che refused to rest on his laurels, he very quickly sensed the coming heaviness of power that gradually stifled the breath of the revolution. He wrote to Peter Marucci, editor of the *Telegraph* in Canada: "Allow me to admit to you that bureaucracy in our country is rock solid and well entrenched and, in its huge bosom, it absorbs paper, incubates it, and sends it to whoever is concerned in its own good time. We carbon-copied the experience of brother countries and that was a mistake, not a terribly serious one, but one that slowed down the free development of our strengths and made a dangerous contribution to one of the phenomena that must be fought most in a socialist revolution, that of bureaucracy."[13] Then, beginning in 1963, Che mounted a crusade against bureaucratism, the advent of which he analyzed not only from an administrative point of view but also a political one, as a phenomenon that gradually interferes with the operation of the state. It is a total shift in the revolutionary society that is in question here. Che observed it and denounced it. The Integrated Revolutionary Organizations, in their first steps towards a unified party, "lost their function of ideological leadership and control of the productive apparatus and became an administrative institution. People without experience and without merit were put in charge of important posts just because they accommodated themselves to the existing situation."[14] The base structures of the revolution, the Committees for the Defense of the Revolution (*Comités de Defensa de la Revolución*—CDR), initially designed to ensure revolutionary fervor, become a "focal point for opportunists who are antipathetic towards the people." Uneasy with the magnitude of the deviation, he ends his article "Against Bureaucratism" on this slogan: "War on bureaucratism. Streamline the state apparatus."[15]

Sometimes Che seemed to limit himself to fighting against bureaucratism because it is a poor method of management, very centralized, and rigid. But gradually he became aware of the danger of the bureaucratization of the Cuban revolution due to the monopoly of power by a privileged caste. It is probable that this rejection of bureaucracy, as it grew stronger, was an additional motive for disagreement with the USSR, kingdom of the *apparatchiks*.

In quitting the Cuban government, Che left political dissatisfaction. His anti-bureaucratic and egalitarian conception had no theoretical result. Viscerally and instinctively hostile to bureaucracy, he did not know how to or could not devise the antidote necessary to put an end to this curse. Hesitantly, for example, he recommended a more conscious participation of each individual and of the people in all operations of the revolution in order to provide a counterweight. He imagined placing the best in the most important posts, hoping himself to make emulators, regretting that "people without experience and without merit were put in charge of important posts just because they accommodated themselves to the existing situation."[16] To Communist youth, he proposed breaking with a vertical and one-sided model that did not have "another line that came the other way and brought communication back from the ranks" and hoped for "a two-way exchange of experiences, ideas, and guidelines."[17]

Che gives the impression of moving forward in his thinking without ever attaining his goal. When he considers a control mechanism to hasten the process of decision making, he only conceives of it from above and rarely from below. However, faced with bureaucracy, only continual and democratic control of decision making by the whole population can serve as a safeguard. To make most of the decisions possible locally, in neighborhoods and workplaces, in regular assemblies, remains the best way to avoid the appropriation of decision making by a social stratum that ends up enjoying this privilege alone. Leaving open the possibility of recalling those elected to sit in assemblies, where all issues that cannot be dealt with locally are decided, makes it possible to avoid any attempt at institutionalization. To limit the number of times a person can be elected to two or three times in a lifetime, and with pay the equivalent of the average wage of the population, is a way to protect against professionalization. Universal suffrage is not the enemy of direct democracy, and multi-party systems and freedom of the press are not the enemies of revolutions, as proven, for example, by the Paris Commune. Rather, it is bureaucracy. There is only one time that Che, in his *Critical Notes on Political Economy,* outlined the main features of democratic planning of the economy.[18]

THE DOCTRINE OF REVOLUTION BY STAGES

Che's conception of the revolution is a radical innovation in relation to the conceptions dominant from the end of the 1920s to the 1960s in the Marxist Left of Latin America. It revives the first period of Latin American Marxism, the period of the "great ancestors": Julio Antonio Mella, founder of Cuban communism, and José Carlos Mariátegui, the first great Marxist thinker of the continent. The latter wrote these prophetic words in 1928: "To capitalist, plutocratic, and imperialist North America, it is not possible effectively to oppose only one socialist America, Latin or Iberian. The era of free competition in the capitalist economy has ended everywhere and in all aspects. We are in the monopoly era, the era of empires. The Latin American countries have arrived late to capitalist competition. The top places have already been permanently assigned. In the capitalist order, the destiny of these countries is to be simple colonies."[19]

After Mariátegui's death in 1930, the Latin American communist parties went in exactly the opposite direction of the one he proposed. This led them to an impasse, despite the devotion, courage, and spirit of sacrifice of numerous generations of militants. There is no doubt that one of the reasons for their historic defeat lies in the false understanding that these parties had of the revolutionary process in the continent, an understanding founded on the theory of "revolution by stages," formulated for the first time by Joseph Stalin in 1927, as a strategy for Chinese communists. In fact, this was just a variant of the Menshevik Party doctrine dating from before October 1917: the conditions in Russia for a socialist revolution are not ripe, it is necessary for the workers' movement to build an alliance with the democratic bourgeoisie to overthrow tsarism and establish a parliamentary democratic republic.

With a few (local or temporary) exceptions, the following principles were, explicitly or implicitly, the foundation of the strategy of the Latin American communist parties throughout their history:

1. The Latin American countries are economically underdeveloped, semi-feudal, and dominated by imperialism. The main contradiction is between the nation and foreign capital (and its internal partners). This contradiction opposes the people allied with the progressive national bourgeoisie (interested in national independent development, industrialization, and the expansion of the internal market) to North American imperialism and its partners, the large landowners (the feudal *latifundistas*).
2. Thus, it is necessary to form a national-democratic front between the popular classes (workers and peasants), the nationalist petite bourgeoisie, and the progressive bourgeoisie. A front that is normally expressed in an electoral alliance between the Communist Party and bourgeois parties is considered to be "patriotic."
3. The Latin American revolution is at the (bourgeois) democratic stage and it has to be carried out by the establishment of a national democratic government supported by the popular masses.
4. The main tasks of this national-democratic revolution are: agrarian reform, expropriation of the large foreign corporations, legalization of workers' parties, and an independent foreign policy.
5. The class struggle between the proletariat and the bourgeoisie is, in the present stage of the revolution, a secondary contradiction. It will only become the principal contradiction at the socialist stage, which will take place in a more or less distant future.

An example of a typical plan that grew out of this rather rigid and dogmatic approach, which Guevara knew well, since it concerned Cuba itself: in August 1960, at the very moment when the Cuban revolution began to expropriate some sectors of the local bourgeoisie and steadily transform itself into a socialist revolution, Blas Roca, Secretary General of the Stalinist Popular Socialist Party (PSP), one of the components of the alliance that had overthrown the Batista dictatorship in 1959, stated during the eighth National Assembly of his party: "The Cuban revolution ...

is a revolution that, given the historic tasks that it confronts and carries out, can rightly be described as a national liberation and agrarian revolution, a patriotic and democratic revolution. . . . The national bourgeoisie, which benefits from the revolution thanks to the increased purchasing power of the people and a greater number of consumers, support the revolution, but are often afraid because of its radical measures and the threats, saber-rattling, and attacks on North American imperialism. . . . Within established limits, it is necessary to guarantee the profits, operation, and national development of private enterprise. It is necessary to stimulate between workers and these companies the enthusiasm to increase productivity."[20]

Confronted with a dynamic revolutionary process that was metamorphosing into socialism, the old Cuban communist leader attempted to enclose it within the limits of the revolution by stages, limits authorized by the Procrustean bed of the Stalinist doctrine.[21] Far from being in the vanguard of the Cuban revolution, in a decisive moment of its development the cadres of the Stalinist PSP attempted, in vain, to put a brake on its radicalization by carrying out a rearguard fight in the name of the "patriotic and democratic" stage.

This is what Che opposed, emphatically and unambiguously, in all his writing on Latin America.

THE NATIONAL BOURGEOISIE

Che's skepticism towards the idea of a "revolutionary bourgeoisie" in Latin America has its initial source in the experiences he accumulated over the course of his numerous trips from 1951 to 1956. In particular, it seems that he was not favorably impressed by what he saw in "national-revolutionary" Bolivia in 1953.

According to the account of his Argentine friend, Ricardo Rojo, who had known him in La Paz, Che made the following caustic (and far-sighted!) commentary on this subject: "This Paz Estensoro is only a reformist who sprays the Indians with DDT to get rid of their lice, but does not resolve the essential problem, which is the cause of the lice. . . . A revolution that does not reach its ultimate consequences is lost."[22]

But, obviously, it was above all the Cuban experience itself that taught him, with great clarity, about the role of the "indigenous" bourgeoisie, panic-stricken before a revolution that is undertaking a radical agrarian reform and is proceeding to expropriate the imperialist monopolies (i.e., the usual tasks of a democratic-national revolution): that bourgeoisie ends up rather rapidly rallying to the counterrevolution.

Che's writings show a clear understanding, without illusions, of the status and role of Latin American national bourgeoisies. He emphasizes their politico-social alliances with the large landowners, alliances that prop up the dominant oligarchy in most countries of the continent, and their close economic, political, ideological, and military links with American imperialism.[23]

That does not mean that there are not secondary contradictions between the interests of the local bourgeoisies and the large North American corporations. But, in the last analysis, each bourgeoisie fears the popular revolution more than the despotic oppression of the foreign monopolies that colonize the economy. For that reason, "a large part of the bourgeoisie opposes revolution openly, and since the beginning has not hesitated to ally itself with imperialism and the landowners to fight against the people and close the road to revolution."[24] This analysis of the behavior of the Latin American bourgeoisie amazingly resembles the analysis Marx made in 1844 of the German bourgeoisie, conservative when it should be revolutionary, fearful when it should be daring, and that was more fearful of the people than of the feudal monarchy that it should have been fighting—a brilliant analysis confirmed by the events of the 1848 German revolution.[25]

Guevara perfectly understood that a revolution of the 1789 type had become impossible in Latin America. In the era of socialist revolution and imperialism, the bourgeoisies that had arrived late on the scene of history could only form a fundamentally conservative force. That became particularly obvious in Latin America after the Cuban Revolution, which polarized the field of the class struggle: "The Cuban Revolution sounded the bell which gave the alarm . . . The majority of national bourgeoisies have united with North American imperialism; thus their fate shall be the same as that of the latter. . . . The polarization of antagonistic forces among class adversaries is up till now more rapid than the development of the contradiction among exploiters over the splitting of the spoils. There are two camps: the alternative becomes clearer for each individual and for each specific stratum of the population."[26]

Che is thus convinced that, contrary to the strategy advocated by the Communist parties, popular forces have no interest in collaborating with the "fearful and treacherous" bourgeoisies that destroy the forces on which they rely in order to accede to power. Furthermore, he is inclined to apply his analysis, not only to the continent, but to the international level as well, noting what he ironically calls the "South Americanization" of the semi-colonial countries of Africa and Asia, i.e., the growing development of a parasitic bourgeoisie that accumulates enormous profits in the shadow of imperialist capital.[27]

Che knew and probably adopted as his own Frantz Fanon's violent indictment against the corruption of the new African bureaucratic bourgeoisie in *The Wretched of the Earth*, a book published in Cuba at the request of Che. There is, moreover, a remarkable affinity between Fanon's thought and Guevara's in several areas: the revolutionary role of the peasantry, the importance of the violence of the oppressed, the anti-imperialist unity of the third world, and the search for a new model of socialism. Che had a great interest in Fanon's work. He conversed with the latter's widow, Josie Fanon, for a long time in Algiers. It is even possible that his reading of Fanon might have been one of the factors that inspired him to participate in the armed struggle in Africa in 1965-1966.

During the writing of his *Critical Notes on Political Economy*, drafted in Prague in 1966, Guevara returns once more to the political role of the bourgeoisie. The Soviet *Manual of Political Economy*, a typical product of Stalinist "Marxism" made by the Academy of Sciences of the USSR, stated: "Concerning the national liberation struggle of the peoples of the colonial and dependent countries, which aims above all to defeat imperialist domination, conquer national independence, and suppress survivals from feudalism, the national bourgeoisie participates in this struggle and plays a certain progressive role." In his commentary, Che rejects this thesis, holding it to be anachronistic: "Historically, that was true, today, it is false. In countries with greater experience of political pseudo-independence, like most Latin American countries, the alliance process between the native bourgeoisies and imperialist capitals was in gestation for a long time. The Cuban Revolution produced a veritable alarm that was heard by the native exploiters. On the other hand, the fight against feudal residues is very problematic because there is also an alliance of the exploiters from diverse sectors and because the large landowners invest in industry and commerce." After having sketched an analogous argument for Africa, he concludes: "The fight against the bourgeoisie is an indispensable condition of the liberation struggle, if one wants to lead it to an irreversibly successful conclusion. (Indonesia is a contrary example)."[28]

THE SOCIALIST CHARACTER OF THE REVOLUTION

If there is no revolutionary bourgeoisie, it is difficult for there to be a bourgeois revolution. Only a socialist revolution founded on an alliance between workers and peasants can accomplish the democratic tasks of the Latin American revolution: agrarian reform, national liberation, and overcoming underdevelopment. It can achieve these goals, not by the bourgeois path, but only by its own methods, which are socialist methods applied to specifically socialist tasks, as in Petrograd in 1917-1919 or Cuba in 1959-1961.

It seems that, already in the Sierra Maestra, Che and some of the guerilla leaders had had the (still vague) intuition of the socialist development of their revolution: "The best among us felt deeply the need for an agrarian reform and an overturning of the social system."[29] The radicalization of the revolution after the seizure of power in 1959 occurred according to a rule that Che knew well: "A revolution which does not constantly expand is a revolution which regresses."[30]

Already in April 1959, in an interview with a Chinese journalist, Che spoke of an "unending development of the revolution" and of the need to abolish the existing "social system" and its "economic foundations."[31] This is exactly what happened in Cuba during the two following years. One wonders from where he got the expression "continuous revolution." Most probably, he invented it himself, from his own experience.

Radicalization of the revolution first occurred through the Cuban agrarian reform that, according to Che, was different from the three other agrarian reforms that had already been tried in America (Mexico, Guatemala, and Bolivia) because of the steadfast will to carry it to its conclusion, without any sort of concession. It was continued by other revolutionary acts, urban reform, expropriation of foreign monopolies, and expropriation of the large Cuban bourgeoisie, acts whose "logical chain . . . carries us forward, step by step, in a progressive and necessary order of concern. . . ."[32] This logic, simultaneously economic, social, and political, is precisely that of the "continuous" (or "permanent") revolution, which leads from the democratic tasks to the socialist tasks, from the fight against imperialism and the *latifundistas* to the fight against their bourgeois allies, from the fall of Batista on January 1, 1959, to the proclamation of the socialist revolution on May 1, 1961. This transformation of the Cuban Revolution—from radical democratic revolution to socialist revolution—poses problems that cannot be reduced to the mechanistic conception of the traditional Latin American Left parties, close to the so-called orthodox Marxist ideas of the Second International[33] such as those of Karl Kautsky or George Plekhanov (the main ideologue of the Mensheviks) for whom underdevelopment and the semi-feudal and semi-colonial character of the economy limited the revolution to the "national democratic stage." In Che's eyes, nothing could be more ridiculous than to "declare, like the theoreticians of the Second International, that Cuba had violated all the laws of the dialectic, of historical materialism, of Marxism." Against this view, or rather Neo-Kautskyan blunder, Che adhered expressly to Lenin, citing the celebrated polemic with the Menshevik historian Soukhanov[34] in order to present the problem in its true terms: Cuba was one of the weakest links of the capitalist world system. It is for this reason that the revolutionary forces in Cuba could ignore the stages of development and "decree the socialist character of the revolution." The revolutionary vanguard, influenced by Marxism, was able to "force the march of events . . . within the limits of what was objectively possible."[35]

Can what was true for Cuba also become true at the level of the continent? In other words, would socialist revolution be the order of the day across Latin America? Beginning in 1961, Che's thought led him towards this conclusion. In his "Message to the Argentines," in May 1962, he speaks explicitly of the socialist revolution as the only true solution for Argentina and the entire continent.[36] In 1963, in *Guerilla Warfare*, he demonstrates the link between the growing social polarization in Latin America and the character of the revolution that looms on the horizon: the increasingly unsustainable contradiction between the exploiters and exploited means that "when the armed vanguard of the people achieves power, both the imperialists and the national exploiting class will be liquidated at one stroke. The first stage of the socialist revolution will have crystallized, and the people will be ready to heal their wounds and initiate the construction of socialism."[37]

Finally, in his "political testament," the Message to the Tricontinental in 1967, Che poses the question in sharp terms, mercilessly bursting all the empty bubbles of Latin American national reformism in the process: "the real liberation of all peoples . . . will, in our America, almost certainly have the characteristic of becoming a socialist revolution. . . . On the other hand, the national bourgeoisies have lost all their capacity to oppose imperialism—if they ever had it—and they have become the last card in the pack. There are no other alternatives; either a socialist revolution or a make-believe revolution."[38]

By taking this position, which follows in the political line of Lenin's *April Theses* and Trotsky's theory of the "permanent revolution," Che synthesized in an audacious, dazzling, and explosive formula the result of the historical experience of popular struggles in the continent and the prediction of the conditions of its liberated future. It will become the flag of the Latin American revolutionary Left throughout the twentieth century.[39]

To what extent is this formula still valid for the other continents of the third world? Che did not formulate a final opinion on this subject, but, in an interview granted to an Algerian journal in March 1965, he explicitly declared: "Socialism or neocolonialism, that is the stake for all of Africa in the encounter now taking place in the Congo."[40] As is well known, a little later in 1965, Che took part in anti-colonialist battles in the Congo at the side of the Lumumbist guerillas commanded by Laurent-Désiré Kabila.

3. *In Search of a New Model of Socialism*

In an article published in 1928, José Carlos Mariátegui, the true founder of Latin American Marxism, wrote these words: "We certainly do not want socialism in the Americas to be a clone or a copy. It has to be an heroic creation. We have to give life, with our own reality, with our own language, to Indo-American socialism. Here is a mission worthy of a new generation."[1] His warning was not heard: in that year, the Latin American communist movement began to fall under the influence of the Stalinist paradigm, which imposed, for almost a half century, the clone and copy of the Soviet bureaucratic ideology, so-called "real socialism."

We do not know if Che knew this text by Mariátegui; it is not impossible that he could have read it, since his companion of the 1950s, the young Peruvian Hilda Gadea, had lent him the writings of the socialist writer.

In any case, it is clear that a good part of his thinking and political practice, above all during the 1960s, had the objective of getting out of the impasse to which the servile imitation of the Soviet and East European model led. His ideas on the construction of socialism are an attempt at the "heroic creation" of something new, the search, continuous and thus incomplete, for a different kind of socialism, radically opposed to the "really existing" bureaucratic caricature in several respects.

From 1959 to 1967, Che's thought continued to evolve. He was increasingly distant from his initial illusions over the USSR and Soviet-style Marxism, that is, Stalinism. In a 1965 letter to his friend, Armando Hart, Cuban Minister of Culture, he strongly criticizes the "ideological imitation" exhibited in Cuba by the publication of Soviet manuals for the teaching of Marxism. He thereby expresses a point of view shared, during the same era, with Fernando Martinez, Aurelio Alonso, and their friends in the Department of Philosophy of the University of Havana and the review *Pensamiento crítico* (Critical Thought). These manuals, which he calls "Soviet cobblestones" (*ladrillos soviéticos*), "have the disadvantage that they leave you nothing to think: the Party has already done it for you and you must digest it."[2]

The murder of Che in October 1967 resulted in the interruption of a process of quite autonomous political maturing and intellectual development. His work is not a closed system, a scaffolding of completed arguments, which has answers for everything. No, on numerous questions, such as democracy in planning or the fight against the bureaucracy, his thinking remains incomplete.[3]

The growing rejection of the "imitate and copy" approach (to borrow Mariátegui's expression) is more explicit in his writings beginning in 1963. So too is his search for an alternative model. He attempts to lay out another path to socialism, more radical, more egalitarian, more fraternal, more human, conforming more to the communist ethic.

The communist ethic for the humanist and revolutionary Guevara was based on essential values: liberty (the liberation from all oppression, political or economic), equality and solidarity (between individuals and peoples), revolutionary democracy, and internationalism.

Three directions concretely express Guevara's aspiration to carve out a new road: the discussion on economic management methods, the question of the free expression of disagreements, and the idea of socialist democracy. The first occupies the principal place in his thinking. The two others, closely linked, are much less developed and they include gaps and contradictions. All three are present in his concerns and his political practice.[4]

METHODS OF ECONOMIC MANAGEMENT

In 1963 and 1964, Guevara, then Minister of Industry, had to confront the partisans of the Soviet model, who wanted to strengthen the financial autonomy of companies, thus allowing the market to work. He entered into the well-known debate on planning, which filled several Cuban economic reviews. In that debate, he was pitted against the Minister of External Commerce, Comandante Alberto Mora, and the Director of the National Institute of Agrarian Reform, Carlos Rafael Rodríguez, former head of the Stalinist Popular Socialist Party (PSP), both of them supported by the Marxist economist and member of the French Communist Party, Charles Bettelheim. Guevara's position in defense of central planning and against market instruments received the support of the Belgian Marxist economist and leader of the Fourth International[5] Ernest Mandel, thus forming, in fact, a radical critique, initially implicit, then more explicit, of "real socialism." The main aspects of the East European model to which he is opposed are:

- The law of value considered as an objective law of economies in transition to socialism;
- Stalin's thesis defended by Charles Bettelheim;
- The commodity as the basis of the productive system;
- Competition, between companies or between workers, as a factor for raising productivity;
- Methods of stimulation and distribution that are individual rather than collective;
- The privileges granted to managers and administrators;
- Market criteria in the economic relations between socialist countries.

In the two years after this debate, Fidel Castro seemed to share a large part of Che's economic theses. Commenting on the Cuban economic discussion, Ernest Mandel made the following observation in 1967: "In our opinion, Che Guevara and Fidel Castro's position is in accordance with Marxist tradition and theory. Those who set out as an absolute principle that the development of the productive forces must occur before socialist consciousness can flourish are just as guilty of mechanistic thinking as those who believe it possible to create such consciousness for the moment through purely subjective means (education, propaganda, agitation, etc.). There is a constant interaction between the creation of a material infrastructure necessary to the growth of socialist consciousness and the development of this consciousness itself."[6]

Very different was Charles Bettelheim's commentary. Close to the "pro-Chinese" circle in the French Communist Party (PCF), he wrote in 1968, in a public exchange with Paul Sweezy, editor of *Monthly Review*, that the theses defended in Fidel's speeches and Che's writings were the expression of a "radicalized fraction of the petite bourgeoisie": the two men are "utopian and dangerous," and their thesis that aims at the disappearance of market relations in socialism is a myth. The entire theoretical operation that tends to oppose planning to the market would inexorably lead to producing ideological obscurantism.[7]

During 1965, Guevara's critique of "real socialism" hardened even more. In the "Speech at Algiers" in February 1965, he demanded that countries that claim to be socialist liquidate "their tacit complicity with the exploiting countries of the West," which resulted in their participation in unequal exchange with the countries of the third world fighting against imperialism. For Che, "there can be socialism only if there is change in man's consciousness that will provoke a new fraternal attitude toward humanity on the individual level in the society which builds or has built socialism and also on a world level in relation to all the peoples who suffer imperialist oppression."[8]

Analyzing the models of building socialism dominant in Eastern Europe in his March 1965 essay "Man and Socialism in Cuba," he rejects the idea that claims "to defeat capitalism with its own fetishes": "Pursuing the wild idea of trying to realize socialism with the aid of the worn-out weapons left by capitalism (the marketplace as the basic economic cell, profit making, individual material incentives, and so forth), one can arrive at a dead end."[9]

In a debate in December 1964, Che returned to the question of the absence of true equality in "real socialism." One of the main dangers of the model imported from the countries of Eastern Europe lies in the strengthening of social inequality and the formation of a privileged stratum of technocrats and bureaucrats: in this system of distribution, "it is the managers who gain more each time. It suffices to look at the latest project of the RDA [*República Democrática Alemana*, Spanish acronym for German Democratic Republic—trans.], the importance of the management made by the manager, or better, the remuneration of the manager."[10] This tendency worried him so greatly that he mentions it again in a letter to Fidel Castro dated April 1965, a little before his departure from Cuba. This letter was published for the first time in 2006, in the work *Critical Notes on Political Economy*, in which he refers to "the material interest of the leaders, the principle of corruption."[11]

Guevara was perfectly aware that his socialist project, founded on planning and not on the "profitability of companies" determined according to the Soviet method of economic motivation, was a *new* attempt, off the beaten track of "real socialism." Reporting his disappointing discussions with the former leaders of the PSP, Carlos Rafael Rodríguez and Blas Roca, and with other partisans of the Soviet model, he notes with regret that the debate could not go very far because the arguments of his opponents only repeated the Soviet *Manual*. To defend the Soviet model, the argument was offered that it had "been of use for more than forty years and, in fact, it is with that model that socialism is built"![12]

Between 1963 and 1966, the partisans of the "law of value in socialism"—Stalin's dogma taken up by Charles Bettelheim in the Cuban economic debate, but contested by Ernest Mandel—and the adepts of the Soviet *Manual* formed a front to defend their economistic view. They posited a conception of the economic sphere as an autonomous system, governed by its own laws, such as the law of value or the laws of the market, against a political and moral conception of socialism, i.e., making economic decisions, such as production priorities, setting prices, etc., according to social, ethical, and political criteria. Guevara's economic proposals turn around several principles: planning against the market, the budgetary system of financing, collective or "moral"[13] incentives, and the like, which set them apart from the Soviet model.

With Stalin, the problem of the law of value in socialism falls within the general context of a metaphysical theory of economic laws in which the laws of science, "be it the laws of nature or the laws of political economy," are the reflection of objective processes that operate independently of human will. These can be discovered, known, and exploited, but they cannot be modified or abolished. This is true whether it "be the period of capitalism or the period of socialism." Consequently, "our enterprises cannot, and must not, function without taking the law of value into account." The latter is, in fact, "a good practical school, which accelerates the development of our executive personnel and their growth into genuine leaders of socialist production," by teaching them "to practice cost accounting and make their enterprises pay."[14]

It is no longer possible cheerfully to disregard everything that distinguishes a natural law from an economic law and everything that separates capitalism, where the "laws of the market" dominate the producers, from socialism, where, according to Marx, human beings consciously control the productive process.

Guevara rebelled against these theses, which he tore to pieces during his discussion with his collaborators in the Ministry of Industry: "Stalin . . . in *The Economic Problems of Socialism in the USSR* . . . spoke of economic laws as something independent of human will, but I want to know how this fundamental law can be converted into a law independent of human will. For me, this is impossible." Certainly, socialism has to satisfy people's needs, but, according to him, "this is not a law": "I consider that economic laws in general must die away in communism and must tend to die away in transition periods." In planning, it is human consciousness that manages society, "certainly in agreement with methods and even certain laws, but these are laws that can be violated, changed, adapted, and created."[15]

The significance of his theses goes far beyond the Cuban economic debate: they outline a novel and "heretical" conception of communism as the "realm of liberty" and as opening an immense field for the emergence of human creativity.

Despite his criticisms of Stalin's economic doctrines, Che did not succeed in formulating a clear idea of the nature of the Stalinist bureaucratic system.

FREEDOM OF DISCUSSION

An important political aspect of the economic debate in 1963-1964 deserves to be brought forward: the very fact that the discussion took place. It does not go without saying that the public expression of disagreements is a normal thing in the process of building socialism. In other words, recognizing and accepting the legitimacy of democratic pluralism in the revolution is not established. This problem, however, remained implicit in the economic debate. Guevara did not develop it explicitly or systematically, particularly in relation to the question of democracy in planning. But his attitude, on various occasions throughout the 1960s, is witness to the fact that he is favorable to free debate and respect for a plurality of opinions. For example, during one of his discussions with his collaborators, in December 1964, he aimed his remarks at his main opponent in the Cuban economic debate, comandante Alberto Mora: "Alberto's work lacks two things: either that he prove to us that we are wrong—which, in any case, would not be bad—or that he show himself to be wrong, which would be not bad either. In either case, something that is rather weak and needs additional work is going to be enriched."[16]

Another interesting example is his behavior towards the Cuban Trotskyists, with whom he in no way agreed: he did not hesitate to criticize them harshly on diverse occasions. In 1961, in an interview with a North American left intellectual, Maurice Zeitlin, Guevara denounced the destruction, by Cuban Stalinists, of the printing plates for Trotsky's work *The Permanent Revolution*, regretting this "error," a thing that "should not have happened." Years later, shortly before leaving Cuba in 1965, he succeeded in getting the Cuban Trotskyist leader Roberto Acosta Hechevarría released from prison. He said, before parting from him with a fraternal embrace, "Acosta, you can't kill ideas with blows."[17]

The most striking example is his response, in a report from 1964, to his comrades in the Ministry of Industry to the criticism of some Soviets, who accused him of defending "pro-Chinese" or, worse yet, "Trotskyist" ideas: "In this regard, I think that either we have the capacity to destroy contrary opinions with arguments or we should let them be expressed.... It is not possible to destroy opinions by force, because that blocks any free development of intelligence. There is much that is worthwhile in Trotsky's thinking, although it seems to me that his fundamental conceptions were wrong and his later action mistaken." Guevara adds ironically that the Soviets applied the label "Trotskyist" to him as a "San Benito," i.e., the habit with which the Inquisition in Spain covered the heretics when leading them to the stake.[18]

It is not, perhaps, by chance that the most explicit defense of freedom of expression and the most direct critique of Stalinist authoritarianism by Guevara appears in the field of art. In his essay *Socialism and Man in Cuba*, he denounced "socialist realism," as an imposed aesthetic line "the functionaries understand." Thus, he emphasized, "true artistic experimentation is annulled" and one straightjacket[s] the artistic expression of the man who is being born and constructed today."[19]

SOCIALIST DEMOCRACY

Che Guevara never worked out a theory of the role of democracy in the transition to socialism. Perhaps this is the greatest lacuna in his work. However, one can assert that he rejected the authoritarian and dictatorial concepts that damaged socialism so much in the twentieth century. To those who claimed to "educate the people" from above, a false doctrine already rejected by Marx in his *Theses on Feuerbach* in 1845 ("it is essential to educate the educator himself"), he responded in a speech in 1960: "The first method for educating the people . . . is to get them to enter into the revolution. You must never pretend to educate a people so that by education alone and a despotic government above, it learns to conquer its rights. Teach it above all to conquer its rights, and this people, once represented in government, will learn everything that can be taught and much more: it will be the master of everything without any effort." In other words, the self-education of people by their own revolutionary practice is the only emancipatory pedagogy, because, as Marx wrote in *The German Ideology*, "in revolutionary activity, the changing of oneself coincides with the transformation of conditions."

The main limit of his thought in this area is an inadequate analysis of the relation between democracy and planning. His arguments in defense of planning against market categories are very important and today take on new relevance in the face of the neoliberal vulgate that led to the triumph of the "religion of the market," but they leave a key political question unanswered: who plans? Who decides the main options of the economic plan? Who determines the priorities of production and consumption? Without a true democracy, without political pluralism, without a free discussion of priorities, and without free choice by the population between several economic proposals and platforms, planning is inevitably transformed into a bureaucratic, authoritarian, and ineffective system of "dictatorship over needs," as the history of the USSR abundantly demonstrates. In other words, the economic problems of the transition towards socialism are inseparable from the nature of the political system. The Cuban experience of the last forty years reveals the negative consequences of the absence of democratic/socialist institutions, even if Cuba succeeded in avoiding the worst bureaucratic and totalitarian aberrations of the other "real socialist" states.

This articulation between politics and economics comes back again to posing the question of revolutionary institutions. Guevara rejects bourgeois democracy but, despite his anti-bureaucratic and egalitarian sensibility, he is far from having a clear vision of the relations between socialism and democracy. In *Socialism and Man in Cuba*, he recognizes that the revolutionary state can be mistaken, thus provoking a negative reaction from the popular masses that obliges it to correct its line. The example he cites is the sectarian policy of the Communist Party under the leadership of the Stalinist Aníbal Escalante in 1961-1962. However, he maintains: "It is evident that the mechanism is not sufficient to assure a sequence of sensible measures. What is missing is a more structured relationship with the masses."[20] Initially, he seems to find a solution in a vague "dialectical interrelation" between the leaders and the masses. However, some pages later, he acknowledges that the problem is far from having found an adequate solution that would allow for effective democratic control: "The institutionalization of the Revolution has still not been achieved. We are searching for something new. . . ."[21]

*

In the last years of his life, Guevara distanced himself a great deal from the Soviet model, rejecting the policy of imitating and copying "real socialism" current in Eastern Europe. His radical critique of the *Manual of Political Economy* of the Academy of Sciences of the USSR,[22] which forms a set of notes composed during his stay in Tanzania and then Prague in 1965-1966, was the strongest expression of this. We have waited a long time, a very long time, for the publication of this document. For dozens of years, it remained outside of circulation: at the very most, a few Cuban researchers were authorized to consult it and cite a few passages from it.[23] It is only today, more than forty years after their writing, that it was decided to publish these notes in Cuba. They are presented in an expanded edition that contains other previously unpublished materials: a letter from Che to Fidel Castro, dated April 1965, which serves as the prologue to the book,[24] notes on writings by Marx and Lenin, a selection of transcriptions of comments exchanged between Guevara and his collaborators during meetings of the Ministry of Industry (already partially published in France and Italy in the 1970s), letters sent to diverse individuals, including Paul Sweezy and Charles Bettelheim, and extracts from an interview with the Egyptian periodical *El-Taliah* in April 1965.

Why were Guevara's notes, often called the "Prague notebook," not published earlier? If absolutely necessary, one can understand that, before the fall of the USSR, there were "diplomatic" reasons for keeping them secret, but after 1991? What "danger" could they represent? The secrecy is truly strange. Who decided that it was necessary to keep them in a drawer? Who finally gave the green light for publication? In the preface to the book, María del Carmen Ariet García of the Centro de Estudios Che Guevara in Havana, the author of an interesting study on Che's political thought, does not offer any explanation and is limited to observing that "this text was, over the years, one of the most anticipated" of Che's works.

This group of notes is now available to interested readers. It testifies both to Guevara's independent spirit and his search for a radical alternative, but it also shows the limits of his thinking.

We begin with this: Che does not understand Stalinism. He attributes the impasses of the USSR in the 1960s to Lenin's New Economic Program (NEP)![25] Certainly, he thinks that, if Lenin had lived longer—he committed the error of dying, Che notes ironically—he would have corrected the effects of the most retrograde aspects of this policy. But he is convinced that the introduction of capitalist elements via the NEP led to harmful tendencies that can be observed in the USSR of 1963, moving in the direction of the restoration of capitalism. All of Guevara's criticisms of the NEP are of interest, and sometimes coincide with those expressed by the Left Opposition from 1923 to 1927. For example, he notes, "the cadres become allied to the system, forming a privileged caste." However, the hypothesis that makes the NEP responsible for the pro-capitalist tendencies in Brezhnev's USSR is manifestly a non-starter. Guevara does not ignore Stalin's harmful role. In one of the critical notes, one can read this precise and striking sentence: "Stalin's terrible historical crime" was "to have scorned communist education and instituted the unlimited cult of authority."[26] This is still not an analysis of the Stalinist phenomenon, although it is already a categorical rejection.

Che employs the term "caste" to refer to the privileged Soviet elite. It is the same one used by Trotsky to designate the bureaucracy. But Trotsky is mentioned nowhere in these critical notes. However, there is another notebook,[27] unpublished, found among Che's papers by Bolivian soldiers—and thus probably written in Bolivia around 1967—which contains numerous extracts from the writings of Lev Davidovitch, notably from *The Permanent Revolution*. Citations from Stalin's works are immediately followed by biting commentary drawn from Trotsky's *The Revolution Betrayed*: "A minor figure against the masses and the revolution, Stalin proved to be the uncontested leader of the Thermidorian bureaucracy, the first of the Thermidorians."[28] There follow several other passages from this work, among them a definition of the bureaucracy as "the privileged and dominant social stratum in Soviet society," a group that has become "an uncontrolled caste, foreign to socialism."[29] It is difficult to know if Che was familiar with these texts, when he used the term bureaucratic "caste" in the *Critical Notes*.

It is appropriate to point out, however, that in most cases it is a matter of secondhand citations, drawn from C. Wright Mills's book *The Marxists*, which appeared in English in 1962, but which Che consulted in the Spanish edition. Moreover, the fact of writing down passages from an author's work in his notebook does not prove that Guevara shared that author's opinion. Still, another part of the notebook contains passages directly drawn from Trotsky's *The History of the Russian Revolution*, a book found by Bolivian soldiers in his backpack. Guevara adds at the end of this part of his notes an explicitly favorable comment: "This is a fascinating book, but from which it is impossible to extract a critique because the historian is also a *protagonist* of the events. In any case, he sheds light on a whole series of events of the great revolution that had remained hidden by myth. At the same time, he makes isolated statements whose validity still remains absolute today. In the last analysis, if one disregards the personality of the author and limits oneself to the book, it must be considered as a source of utmost importance for the study of the Russian Revolution."[30]

Let us return to his comments on the Soviet *Manual.* Most of Guevara's criticisms closely correspond to his economic writings in the 1963-1964 period: the defense of central planning against both the law of value and "self-managed" factories, that is, ones that are autonomous and function according to the rules of the market; and the defense of communist education against individual monetary incentives. He is also worried, and rightly so, about the profit-sharing schemes of the factory managers, which he considers to be a principal source of corruption.

Guevara considers planning to be the central axis of the process of constructing socialism because it "liberates the human being from the condition of being an economic thing." He recognizes, in the letter to Fidel, that in Cuba "the workers do not participate in making the plan." Who should plan? The debate of 1963-1964 had not responded to that question. In Guevara's critical notes of 1965-1966, several passages clearly pose the principle of a socialist democracy in which the people themselves make the important economic decisions. The masses, he writes, must participate in the formulation of the plan while its execution is a purely technical affair. In the USSR, in his opinion, the plan, conceived as "an economic decision of the masses, conscious of their role," was surreptitiously replaced by a mechanism in which the economic levers determine everything. The masses, he insists, "should have the possibility to direct their own destinies, to decide how much is going to accumulation and how much to consumption"; economic technology should work with these figures, decided by the people, and "the consciousness of the masses should ensure its accomplishment." This subject returns on several occasions: the workers, he writes, the people in general, "will settle the important problems of the country (rates of growth, accumulation/consumption)," even if the plan itself will be the work of specialists. This separation between economic decisions and their execution is too mechanical and can be questioned. But, by these formulations, Guevara is getting considerably closer to the ideal of democratic socialist planning, such as Ernest Mandel formulated it, for example. He does not draw all the political conclusions—democratization of power, political pluralism, freedom of organization—but the importance of this new vision of economic democracy cannot be denied.

These notes, which were inaccessible for a long time, are undeniably an important stage in Guevara's path towards a communist and democratic alternative to the Stalinist model of the Soviet Union.

4. *The Guevarist Heritage in Latin America*

Che, like José Martí, Emiliano Zapata, Augusto Sandino, Farabundo Martí, and Camilo Torres, is a figure who fell while standing with weapons in hand and became a star in the sky of popular hope, a burning coal beneath the ashes of disenchantment.

CHE'S PRESENCE IN LATIN AMERICA TODAY

Since the 1960s, a specter haunts the sleep of the powerful and inspires the dreams and struggles of the oppressed in Latin America: "Guevarism." Is there a revolutionary or radical opposition movement on the continent, even at the beginning of the twenty-first century, that does not claim to follow, to one degree or another, the Argentine doctor and guerilla?

The years go by, fashions change, modernisms are succeeded by postmodernisms, dictatorships are replaced by low-intensity democracies, the Berlin Wall is replaced by the wall of money, Keynesianism is replaced by neoliberalism. However, Guevara's message, forty years later, contains a glowing ember that continues to burn.

Something in the life and message of the Argentine-Cuban doctor-guerilla still speaks to today's generation. If not, how to explain the plethora of books, articles, films, and discussions? It is not the simple effect of commemorating the fortieth anniversary of his death. Who was interested, in 2003, in the fiftieth anniversary of Joseph Stalin's death?

Are not Che's ideas out of date? Would it now be possible to change Latin American societies, in which an oligarchy that has been in power for several centuries monopolizes resources, wealth, and weapons while exploiting and oppressing the people, without a revolution? This is the thesis that has been defended for twenty years by the ideologues of the "realist" Left in Latin America, such as the writer and journalist Jorge Castañeda in his book *Utopia Unarmed: The Latin American Left after the Cold War*, which was published in 1993. It is an irony of history that, some months after the publication of this book, Mexico experienced the spectacular uprising of the indigenous inhabitants of Chiapas under the leadership of an armed utopian organization, the Zapatista Army of National Liberation (EZLN—*Ejército Zapatista de Liberación Nacional*), whose main leaders claimed to have Guevarist roots. Castañeda was, partially, refuted: it is true that the Zapatistas, contrary to traditional guerilla groups, do have not the objective of taking power, but of inciting the self-organization of the oppressed with a view to a profound transformation of the social and political system of their country.[1]

The EZLN became, over the course of the 1980s, the "organic" expression of the indigenous communities of Chiapas. While a Guevarist component is indeed present from the birth of the group that formed the EZLN, the movement favored, after the insurrectional act of 1994, political action and the mobilization from below of "civil society" against the authoritarian regime of the Mexican state. Nevertheless, without the uprising of January 1994, the EZLN, still with weapons in hand thirteen years later, would not have become an example for the victims of neoliberalism, not only in Mexico, but throughout Latin America and the entire world. Although neo-Zapatismo combines several subversive traditions, Guevarism is the essential ingredient of this seething and unforeseen revolutionary culture, be it through the formation of an "army of liberation," the choice of the rifle as the material expression of the defiance of the oppressed towards the state and the dominant classes, the emphasis on forging a direct link between the combatants and the peasant masses (the indigenous population), or the radical prospect of anticapitalist struggle. We are far from the Bolivian adventure of 1967, but close to the revolutionary ethic incarnated in Che. Through its libertarian sensibility, its self-irony, its rejection of power, and its internationalist appeal to fight against neoliberalism, the EZLN has given rise to an extensive echo that reaches well beyond the borders of Mexico.

In fact, the heritage of Guevarism, as revolutionary sensibility, as unwavering resistance to the dictatorship of capital, and as a socialist perspective, is an enduring presence in the radical Left of Latin America. One example: in 2006, the Manuel Rodríguez Patriotic Front (FPMR—*Frente Patriotico Manuel Rodriguez*), Guevarist dissident group of the Chilean Communist Party that had organized an attack against the dictator Augusto Pinochet in September 1986, convened a meeting in Santiago of different Latin American organizations claiming to draw inspiration from Che's ideas.

More significant is the influence of Guevarism in several mass social movements, such as the MST, Brazil's *Movimento dos Trabalhadores Rurais Sem Terra* (Landless Rural Workers' Movement). Born in 1984 as a result of the long years of the Catholic Church's support for consciousness raising and promoting of peasant self-organization through its Pastoral Land Commission, the MST sprang up within the Liberation Theology movement, but rapidly became an autonomous and non-confessional movement rallying hundreds of thousands of militants. It is undoubtedly the most important and most combative social movement in Brazil today. Its objective has always been agrarian reform, but the MST also demands a radical change in the country's neoliberal development model and the beginning of a more just society "without exploited or exploiters" (MST's Charter of Principles).

Guevara is one of the main political reference points for the MST and a source of inspiration for the "mystique" of the movement: its radical aspirations and the dedication of its militants to the cause of social justice. Many of them have paid with their lives for their commitment to fighting the *latifundistas*. To be sure, the MST is not an armed movement and guerilla warfare is not part of its method of struggle. But it does not hesitate to transgress the law and the sacrosanct principle of private property through its massive occupations of land. Che's ethic and his program for the revolutionary emancipation of Latin America is the foundation of its socio-political culture.

Guevara's ideas are also present, in a more diffuse way, in a number of Latin American social movements, from the Argentine *piqueteros* to the Bolivian workers, the native Mapuches of Chile to the Mayas of Guatemala. With the exception of the Colombian ELN (*Ejército de Liberación Nacional*), there are no longer Guevarist organizations leading an armed struggle in the countryside. Henceforth, for these movements as well as for people from one end of the continent to the other, Che does not symbolize a method of rural guerilla warfare, but a certain *spirit*, both ethical and political, formed from revolt against the domination of imperialism, rage against capitalist social injustice, intransigent struggle against the established order, and the intense desire for a socialist and revolutionary transformation of society. That is also true for the new generation of students discovering Guevara's writings, on their own or thanks to motivated teachers. The most striking example is Argentina, where there is a network of "Che Guevara" chairs around the People's University of the Mothers of May Square (*Asociaciòn Madres de Plaza de Mayo*), under the leadership of Claudia Korol and Néstor Kohan.

What about Bolivia, the country where Guevara shed his blood? At the beginning of the twenty-first century, the country experienced a spectacular growth of social movements, led by the native population and the peasantry, notably coca farmers (a leaf traditionally chewed by Bolivians, not to be confused with cocaine), and by the populations of the shantytowns, such as El Alto, on the heights above La Paz. These movements carried out the "gas war" against the petroleum multinationals and overthrew the neoliberal governments that had become subject to them. Hence, we witnessed presidents Gonzalo Sáchez de Lozado, in 2003, and Carlos Mesa, in 2005, dismissed by genuine popular uprisings. Evo Morales, leader of the coca growers' union (the *cocaleros*) and the founder of the *Movimiento al Socialismo* (MAS—Movement for Socialism), was elected in 2005 to the Presidency of the Republic. During his inauguration speech in January 2006, he paid homage to "our ancestors who fought: Tupak Katari to restore the *Tahuantinsuyo*, Simón Bolívar who fought for this great homeland, and Che Guevara who fought for a new world in equality."[2] Among the members of his government are militants who fought alongside Che in the Bolivian ELN (*Ejército de Liberación Nacional de Bolivia*), like Loyola Guzmán.

More paradoxical is the case of Venezuela. Hugo Chávez, an ex-soldier democratically elected and reelected, has taken on two decisive parts of the Guevarist program: "Bolivarian" anti-imperialist unity of the Latin American peoples and the socialist perspective. The Bolivarian revolution that has been developing in Venezuela for the last few years satisfies a profound desire for change. In 1989, a popular semi-insurrection in Caracas against the corrupt regime and the neoliberal policies of president Carlos Andrés Pérez had been bloodily suppressed, producing hundreds of casualties. In protest, a group of leftist army officers led by Hugo Chávez attempted a military uprising in 1992, which failed. Imprisoned and then amnestied two years later, Chávez was triumphantly elected president in 1998. He escaped an attempted *coup d'état* orchestrated by Washington that failed due to a massive popular mobilization. In his numerous speeches in defense of twenty-first-century socialism, Guevara occupies a prime place. The charismatic Venezuelan president can also be considered an heir to the leftist currents among the Venezuelan military who had, at the beginning of the 1960s, attempted several uprisings inspired by the Cuban Revolution and ended up, in part, by joining rural guerilla groups.[3]

It is still too early to know what direction these two governments, undoubtedly the most left in contemporary Latin America, are going to take. They contrast strongly with those of the "center-left" in Brazil (Luiz Inácio da Silva), Uruguay (the Frente Amplio), and Chile (Michèle Bachelet), which are converts to social-liberalism. All of them bear witness, each in its own way, to the relevance of the ideas of the fighter murdered in October 1967.

Cuba is a case apart. After a long eclipse, during the years of economic, political, and ideological alignment with the USSR (1969-1986), there has been a renewed interest in Che, and not only as a symbol of the heroic guerilla. Due to the work that Carlos Tablada has devoted to his economic thought, to the accounts collected by Orlando Borrego, the brilliant essays of Fernando Martínez Heredia, and the spirited writings of Celia Hart, Guevara's thought is again being included in the political and intellectual discussion of the island. Not to mention the long anticipated Cuban publication in 2006 of Guevara's notebook of unpublished critical notes on political economy.

In all manifestations of the revolutionary movement in Latin America today, traces of "Guevarism," sometimes visible, sometimes invisible, can be perceived. They are present in the collective imagination of militants, in their discussions about methods, strategy, and the nature of the struggle. They can be considered seeds that have germinated over the last fifteen years in the political culture of the Latin American Left, producing branches, leaves, and fruits. Or they can be considered one of the red threads with which, from Patagonia to the Rio Grande, dreams, utopias, and revolutionary actions are woven.

THE YEARS OF COMBAT

Guevarism's reception today differs in several respects from that of the years of combat, between 1960 and 1979, which saw the growth of a guerilla warfare movement that claimed to follow in Che's footsteps. These fights left profound traces in the history of the continent, traces that the powerful have sought to efface from memory by all means. Hence, there is all the more reason to recall these combatants who should never be forgotten.

During that period, Latin America was subjected to the overwhelming economic, political, and military domination of the American Empire, which intervened on several occasions, directly by sending troops and by encouraging military *coups d'état*. The peasant masses, that is, the majority of the population, were turned over to the brutal power of the large landowners and social inequalities were widened in conjunction with economic "development." In these explosive social conditions, the Cuban Revolution and its steady evolution toward socialism could not but have a very sizable impact: a series of movements in several countries of Latin America attempted to follow the example of the guerilla campaign of the Sierra Maestra. This is the case with the armed struggle in Venezuela, led by the dissident communist Douglas Bravo, in Peru with the MIR (*Movimiento izquierdo revolucionario*—Revolutionary Left Movement) founded by Luis de la Puente Uceda (who was killed by the army in 1965), or in Colombia, around the *Ejército de Liberación Nacional* (ELN—National Liberation Army), in which the priest Camilo Torres participated. He died in a confrontation with the military in 1966. Che's *Guerilla Warfare* and his 1967 "Message to the Tricontinental" contributed much to the formation of this current, whose most important expression was the Congress of the Organization of Latin American Solidarity (OLAS) on August 1, 1967, in Havana.

Paradoxically, it is only after his defeat and death in Bolivia that the guerilla doctor became the main political and moral reference point for the revolutionary Left in Latin America, the example and ideal whom those who took up arms against the dictatorships in Brazil, Chile, Uruguay, Bolivia, and Central America claimed to follow. As Walter Benjamin wrote in thesis XII of *Theses on the Philosophy of History*, it is the memory of defeated and martyred ancestors that inspires the present struggle of the oppressed classes.

Brazil was one of the first countries in which Guevarism gave rise to the appearance of several armed leftist organizations engaged in resistance against the military dictatorship established in 1964. Among the most important: the *Ação Libertadora Nacional* (ALN—National Liberation Action), led by a veteran communist cadre, Carlos Marighella, who had broken with the Brazilian Communist Party and participated in the OLAS Congress in Havana; and the *Movimento Revolucionário 8 de Outubro* (MR-8—Revolutionary Movement 8th October), which was named to pay tribute to the day of Guevara's murder. Captain Carlos Lamarca, an officer of the regular army who had passed, literally with weapons and kit, to the side of the resistance, led it for some time. After a series of spectacular actions in the 1968-1971 period—banks robbed, the American ambassador taken hostage and exchanged for dozens of political prisoners, and weapons stolen from barracks—these organizations were destroyed by the police and the Brazilian army and their members arrested and tortured. Marighella fell in an ambush in 1969 and Lamarca in a confrontation in 1971.

In the other countries of the continent during the 1970s, the "somber years" of the Latin American dictatorships, a wide range of Guevarist politico-military groups arose, whose key figures included Raúl Sendic, founder of the *Movimiento de Liberación Nacional Tupamaros* (MLN—National Liberation Movement Tupamaros) in Uruguay; Miguel Enríquez, the main leader of the Chilean MIR (*Movimiento de Izquierda Revolucionaria*—Revolutionary Left Movement); and Roberto Santucho of the *Partido Revolucionario de Trabajo-Ejército Revolucionario del Pueblo* (PRT-ERP—Revolutionary Workers' Party-Revolutionary Army of the People) in Argentina. In 1972, during a meeting of the representatives of these three organizations, each counting thousands of members and combatants, Miguel Enríquez advanced the idea of creating an international organization, a "small Zimmerwald" in his words, in memory of the Swiss city where, in 1915, the few representatives of the internationalist Left, opponents of the imperialist war, met. This proposal was accepted by the two other groups and soon after the Bolivian ELN (*Ejército Liberación Nacional*—National Liberation Army), founded by Che and led by the Peredo brothers, joined the initiative. After a period of consolidating their relations, the formation of the *Junta de coordinación revolucionaria* (JCR—Junta for Revolutionary Coordination), composed of the four organizations, was proclaimed at the beginning of 1974. The red flag of the JCR displayed Che's image, symbol of their joint liberation struggle. Unlike OLAS, the JCR was not an initiative of the Cuban leadership, even if it had fraternal links with the latter. The formation of this alliance marked the growth of a certain autonomy of Latin American Guevarism in relation to Cuba.

The JCR's appeal "To the Peoples of Latin America" of April 1974 was an impressive document, which had a profoundly radical and subversive vision for the whole continent. The formation of the Junta was presented as an important step towards "the concretization of one of the principal strategic ideas of comandante Che Guevara, hero, symbol, and precursor of the continental socialist revolution." It was a matter of organizing the struggle for "the second independence, towards final national and social liberation, towards the final elimination of the unjust capitalist system, and towards the establishment of revolutionary socialism."[4]

Even though they had some support in the countryside, these armed movements were essentially urban. They gained significant support among student and intellectual youth, in certain impoverished neighborhoods, and in the radicalized sectors of the working class. The PRT was established in class unions, the MIR in the population, and the Tupamaros in the struggles of workers and peasants. However, they remained minority vanguards, sometimes too militarized. Victims of the ruthless repression of the military dictatorships of the Southern Cone, the organizations were decimated by torture and murders: thousands of victims in Chile, tens of thousands of "disappeared" in Argentina, a true crime against humanity that remains unpunished. Around 1977, the Junta for Revolutionary Coordination had practically ceased to exist, its main leaders killed (Miguel Enríquez and Roberto Santucho) or imprisoned in degrading conditions (Raúl Sendic). In fact, it was an entire generation of young people who sacrificed their lives or freedom in an unequal fight against the steamroller of the dictatorships, actively supported by the North American government, the Pentagon, and the CIA. Undoubtedly, they were mistaken, their strategy was not the best nor their tactics. They were too militarized and too "vanguardist." However, the generosity, dedication, courage, and authentic revolutionary aspirations that carried them into combat cannot be denied, nor can the moral and political legitimacy of their resistance to the sinister dictatorships of the Southern Cone.

Furthermore, if the tragic experience of Chile in September 1973 is taken into consideration, were not the Guevarist militants and those of the Chilean revolutionary Left in general right in long calling for the arming of the workers to face a military *coup*? Their watchword was "*El pueblo armado jamás será aplastado*" (An armed people will never be crushed). While Luis Corvalán, Secretary-General of the Chilean Communist Party, explained in a quite learned fashion that it was necessary to have confidence in the constitutional and democratic traditions of the Chilean armed forces.

Some ex-militants of this generation, converted to social-liberalism, now maintain that Che and the Guevarists of South America were motivated by "suicidal impulses." Nothing is further from the truth. Che, Miguel Enríquez, or Roberto Santucho loved life passionately. They undoubtedly committed mistakes, underestimated the risks and a balance of power that was unfavorable to them. But their action was not at all suicidal. To the contrary, they acted out of a feeling of duty, at the risk of their lives, for a just and humane cause. During all of the years of guerilla warfare and armed struggle in Latin America, there was not a single case of a suicide attack or kamikaze action.

Guevarism also exerted influence over other political currents, giving rise to dissidence in several communist, socialist, and populist (in the Latin American sense of the term) parties, such as the Peruvian APRA (*Alianza Popular Revolucionaria Americana*—American Popular Revolutionary Alliance), from which Luis de la Puente, Guillermo Lobatón, and their comrades in the MIR originated. Christians of the Left, and later liberation theology, were also attracted by the martyr figure of Che, an attraction that was all the stronger in that several members of the clergy were involved in revolutionary action, such as Camilo Torres and his successor in the leadership of the Colombian ELN, the Spanish priest José Pérez.

The Trotskyist current has also experienced the impact of Guevarism, and not only in Latin America. The *Jeunesse communiste révolutionnaire* (Revolutionary Communist Youth), created in France in 1965, had one of its main political and moral reference points in the thought and action of Che. Janette Habel, one of the founders of this organization (precursor of the current *Ligue communiste revolutionnaire*—Revolutionary Communist League), who was to go on to play an important role in May 1968, stated during a conference of solidarity with Vietnam in Berlin in February 1968: "The youth of Western Europe should be inspired by Che's example, the revolutionary without frontiers. We must defend Che like a flag . . . , defend his concept of the new human being, who is involved in the anti-imperialist fight, his conception of the revolutionary human being, who is sensitive to the fate of all the exploited and fights, without waiting for any material reward for his or her efforts, by opposing revolutionary violence to reactionary violence."[5]

In Bolivia, the Trotskyists of the *Partido Obrero Revolucionario* (POR—Revolutionary Workers' Party), led by Hugo González Moscoso, called for supporting Che's guerilla column in 1967 and attempted, in vain, to make contact with it. In the years 1968-1971, the POR and the Guevarist ELN established links of close political and military cooperation. One of the leaders of the POR, Tomás Chambi, was killed in 1971 while fighting against the *coup d'état* of General Banzer. In Chile, the Trotskyists, notably the historian Luis Vitale, participated in the founding of the MIR in 1965. As for the Argentine PRT (*Partido revolucionario de los trabajadores*—Workers' Revolutionary Party), during the initial period of its existence, up until 1972, it was the Argentine section of the Fourth International. Moreover, the latter had approved a resolution, during its Ninth World Congress in 1969, favorable towards armed struggle in Latin America, while defending the political role of vanguard parties against the strictly "focoist" conception of combat. In Brazil, the *Partido Operário Comunista* (POC—Communist Workers' Party), a partisan of this politico-military orientation, was also a member of the Fourth International, but was destroyed by repression after one of its principal leaders, the young Luis Eduardo Merlino, was killed under torture by police in 1971.

Of course, the Guevarists were not the only ones to carry out guerilla warfare and armed struggle. Communist parties, such as the *Fuerzas Armadas Revolucionarias de Colombia* (FARC—Revolutionary Armed Forces of Colombia), for example, and Maoist organizations, particularly in Brazil and Colombia, also carried out struggles of this type, but generally with a more national-democratic than socialist program and with different methods. We leave aside the strange case of the *Sendero Luminoso* (SL—Shining Path), a Peruvian Maoist group that slid into a blind violence of the Pol Pot type.

Attempting to draw up a balance sheet of the first Guevarist wave, from 1967 to 1977, in the semi-industrialized countries of the Southern Cone, one can only notice that all these movements failed to overthrow the dictatorships. They practically disappeared under the blows of political and military repression, except for the Tupamaros in Uruguay, and that at the price of a profound political transformation.

While Guevarism was defeated everywhere in the Southern Cone, the balance sheet in the still largely agrarian countries of Central America, like Cuba in the 1950s, is more uneven. Here Guevarist guerilla movements, by markedly altering their political and military strategy, obtained significant results, notably in Nicaragua and, to a lesser extent, in El Salvador and Guatemala. The *Frente Sandinista de Liberación Nacional* (FSLN—Sandinista National Liberation Front) went beyond the focoist conception to a broader and more varied approach, combining rural guerilla and urban actions, political work in poor neighborhoods, local insurrections, political alliances, and mass strikes. But if the path of armed uprising had not been chosen, under the influence of Guevarism, the Somoza dictatorship would not have been overthrown in July 1979. In El Salvador, the *Frente Farabundo Martí de Liberación Nacional* (FMLN—Farabundo Martí National Liberation Front) succeeded over the course of the 1980s in becoming a political and military force deeply rooted in the poor and excluded strata in the cities and countryside. Even if it could not, like the Nicaraguan FSLN, "take power" because of the military support of the United States for the local dictatorship, it was able to impose through the peace accords a certain democratization of the country. An analogous process took place in Guatemala, where several guerilla movements with a Guevarist tendency, including the *Ejército Guerrillero de los Pobres* (EGP—Guerilla Army of the Poor), united into the *Unidad Revolucionaria Nacional Guatemala* (UNRG—Guatemalan National Revolutionary Unity) had negotiated agreements, but with more disappointing results. With the defeat of the Sandinistas in the Nicaraguan elections of 1990 and the signing of the peace agreement in El Salvador in 1992, the cycle of guerilla wars in Central America came to an end.[6]

How did this generation, engaged in armed struggle against the dictatorships, change after the reestablishment of democracy in Latin America in the 1980s and 1990s? Some, above all those who were close to the social movements, remained faithful to their ideals of revolutionary change, even if the methods of struggle changed. Others, linked to institutionalized practices of the state, notably in Brazil, evolved towards reformism and social liberalism. Between these two poles are found a whole range of intermediate options.

Among those who had a change of heart, there is one who merits a place in an updated version of *The Universal History of Infamy* by Jorge Luis Borges: the one named Joaquín Villalobos, who was the main leader of the ERP (*Ejército Revolucionario del Pueblo*—Revolutionary Army of the People) of El Salvador, one of the armed organizations that developed in the country during the 1970s. Roque Dalton was one of the members of the ERP, a communist militant and brilliant poet and writer. After many years of exile in Cuba, he returned to El Salvador to participate in the armed struggle. In 1975, under the leadership of Joaquín Villalobos, Roque Dalton was tried by his comrades, condemned as an "agent of the CIA" or a "Cuban agent," and executed in May 1975. This charge was ridiculous and was not accepted by the Latin American Left. As a result of his death, the revolutionary movement lost one of its most human and captivating figures. After the signing of the peace agreements in El Salvador in 1992, Joaquín Villalobos converted rapidly to social-liberalism. Settled in England, he supported the government of Tony Blair.

Not everyone has opted for capitulation, far from it. Among those who have remained faithful to their youthful ideals, some have been able to find new forms in which to pursue the fight for the liberation of the oppressed, such as the founders of the EZLN in Chiapas.

5. *From Internationalism to Alterglobalism, from the Tricontinental to the Intercontinental*

CHE'S INTERNATIONALISM

For Che, revolutionary internationalism was not a subject to be reserved for edifying speeches on May Day. Just as for the founders of the Communist International, it was simultaneously a way of life, a supreme ideal, a secular faith, a categorical imperative, and a spiritual homeland. The significance of Che's internationalism can only be understood in the light of his revolutionary humanism.[1]

Internationalism is a strategic imperative in the fight against imperialism. (This is the central theme of Che's "Message to the Tricontinental" in 1967.) It is also a high moral requirement: an internationalist is one who experiences "any attack on, any affront to human dignity and happiness anywhere in the world as a personal affront."[2]

Obviously, internationalism must not only be felt. Above all, it must be practiced through real and effective solidarity with people who are fighting against imperialism and through economic and military aid from socialist countries to nations that have embarked on their own struggle for liberation. Inspired by these principles, Che, in his famous and sensational speech delivered in February 1965 in Algiers, calls on the industrialized socialist countries not to organize trade with the underdeveloped countries on the ground of the unequal exchange relations established on the basis of the law of value.

Internationalism is not only a moral imperative for consistent communism, the true political manifestation of humanist values, but also, and above all, a practical and real necessity in the revolutionary struggle against the common imperialist enemy.

A GLOBAL STRATEGY AGAINST IMPERIALISM

Guevara quickly became aware of the continental nature of the struggle, of which the Cuban Revolution was the first milestone. In his "Message to Argentines" of May 25, 1961, the anniversary of the anti-colonial rebellion that shook Argentina in 1910, Che recalls the historical precedent of the continental level struggles against Spanish tutelage in the nineteenth century and insists on the reciprocal aid that the armed rebels of the various Latin American countries had given each other. He thus revived the "Bolivarian" tradition of Latin America, giving it, however, a proletarian and socialist content.[3]

But it was probably the Cuban missile crisis of October 1962 and the imminent threat of an American invasion of the island that put the continental revolution at the center of his concerns. In an essay written during this period, "Tactics and Strategy of the Latin American Revolution," Che affirmed his belief that the United States would always intervene, sooner or later, against Latin American revolutions to maintain its dominant influence in the region. He concludes that there is a need for an organized response on the continental level: "Given this overall panorama of Latin America, we find it difficult to believe that victory can be achieved in one isolated country. The union of repressive forces must be countered with the unity of the popular forces. In every country where oppression reaches the limits of tolerance, the banner of rebellion must be raised, and this banner will, of historical necessity, be continental in character. The Andean Cordilleras are destined to be the Sierra Maestra of America, as Fidel has said, and all the immense territories of this continent are destined to be the scene of a struggle to death against imperialist power."[4]

As far as the Bolivian guerilla war of 1967 is concerned, it is known that Guevara saw it precisely as the first stage of a continental revolution, of which Peru and Argentina should be the priority focus, followed later by Paraguay and Brazil. Che was clearly aware that the Latin American revolution itself was only part of a larger movement of "humanity [that] has said 'enough' and has begun to move," according to an expression taken from the last phrase of the Second Declaration of Havana, which became the watchword of the Tricontinental.

His interest in the worldwide dimension of the war against imperialism had developed from his first diplomatic trips through the countries of the third world in 1959. In an article published in the Mexican review *Humanismo* in September 1959, Che had already defined anti-imperialist solidarity in terms of a Marxist class analysis, i.e., proletarian internationalism: "Could it be that our brotherhood transcends distances, different languages, and the absence of close cultural links, and unites us in the struggle? Should a Japanese worker be closer to an Argentine laborer, a Bolivian miner, the man working for United Fruit Company, or the Cuban sugar cutter than to a Japanese samurai?"[5]

But the factor that most contributed to the formation of his international strategic perspective was the revolutionary war of the Vietnamese people. Che belonged to a generation for whom the war in Vietnam played the same polarizing role as the Spanish Civil War had for an earlier generation. It was a genuine revelation, crystallizing internationalist consciousness around it at the world level. Already in 1963, following the first great development of the National Liberation Front (NLF) guerilla organization, Che emphasized that the Vietnamese were "front-line soldiers in the front trenches of the world proletariat against imperialism" and that their front of the struggle was extremely important for the whole future of America.[6] And it is of Vietnam that he is thinking when he proclaimed in Algiers in 1965: "There are no frontiers in this struggle to the death. We cannot remain indifferent in the face of what occurs in any part of the world. A victory for any country against imperialism is our victory, just as any country's defeat is a defeat for all. The practice of proletarian internationalism is not only a duty for the peoples who struggle for a better future, it is also an inescapable necessity."[7]

It was after 1965, during the American escalation, the open and massive intervention of the imperialist army in Vietnam, that Guevara formulated in an explicit and precise manner his global revolutionary strategy, whose first public expression was the "Message to the Tricontinental" in 1967. In this dazzling and incisive text, Che specifically refers to the following subjects:

- Imperialism, the highest stage of capitalism, is a world system, and it is necessary to fight it in a vast and prolonged global confrontation.
- To fight against the common enemy of the human race, American imperialism, the socialist countries and their supporters must unite their efforts, despite their differences. The current form that these differences take is a weakness, but the necessary unity will ultimately impose itself under the pressure of the enemy's blows.
- In this gigantic struggle, the historic task of the peoples of the third world is to eliminate the bases of subsistence for imperialism in the underdeveloped countries, which are sources of profit and raw materials, markets for products from the countries of the center, and today subjected to an absolute dependence.
- Today, there needs to be a global strategy for the war against imperialism, capable of effectively aiding the vanguard detachment of the world proletariat: Vietnam. It is necessary to create two, three, many Vietnams so as to force imperialism to disperse its forces.

This was the first time, in a very long time, that a Communist leader of worldwide stature tried to outline an international revolutionary strategy that was not the function of a state's interests. In this sense also, Che's thought signifies a return to the sources, to the Communist International of the early years (1919-1924), before it gradually became an instrument in the service of the foreign policy of Stalin's USSR.

On the other hand, this appeal was not an abstract and platonic wish. It was written from the depths of the Bolivian forest by a man who tried to accomplish what he advocated and who sacrificed his life for this goal: to come to the aid of the Vietnamese people by opening a second front in Latin America. This explains the resounding echo of the document around the globe.

The appeal was intended for the Organization of Solidarity with the People of Asia, Africa, and Latin America. Its central focus was on the role of the people of these three continents. That does not mean, however, that Che's conception was a vague "third-worldism," without any clear political content. Nothing is more false than the thesis, spread by certain superficial and dubious interpreters, that for Che "the real contradiction was not between capitalism and communism, but between developed and underdeveloped countries."[8] For Guevara, the worldwide revolution against imperialism was conceived in terms of a class analysis and its ultimate aim was, without a shadow of a doubt, the establishment of communism on a world scale. Moreover, while recognizing that the combativeness of the workers of the imperialist countries had grown weaker, he never fell into an anti-European nihilism. In fact, Che predicted, in the appeal to the Tricontinental, that in Europe "the contradictions would, in the next few years, reach an explosive level" (and this was not even a year before May 1968!) and that the class struggle would, in the end, burst out in the very heart of the American capitalist center.

In his criticisms of the foreign policy pursued by the countries of "real socialism," Che also championed internationalism. This critique brings us back to his *Critical Notes on Political Economy*. While the authors of the official work of the USSR Academy of Sciences praise "mutual aid" between socialist countries, the former Cuban Minister of Industry is obliged to note that this does not correspond to reality: "If proletarian internationalism directed the acts of the governments of each socialist country . . . , it would be a success. But internationalism is replaced by chauvinism (of the great power or the small country) or by submission to the USSR. . . . That injures all the honest dreams of the world's communists." A few pages later, in an ironic commentary on the assertion of the Soviet *Manual of Political Economy* that the division of labor between socialist countries is based on "fraternal collaboration," Guevara observes: the "CMEA[9] is a hornets' nest and refutes this assertion in practice. The text refers to an idea that could be established only through a true practice of proletarian internationalism, but that is lamentably absent today." Another passage notes with bitterness that in the relations among countries claiming to be socialist there is "expansionism, unequal exchange, competition, up to a certain point exploitation, and certainly submission of weak states to the strong." Finally, when the *Manual* recalls the necessity for the state to "build communism," the critique poses this rhetorical question: "Can communism be built in a single country?"[10] Another interesting remark offers a similar observation: Lenin, Che observes, "clearly affirmed the universal character of the revolution, which was then denied."[11] This is a transparent reference to the policy of "socialism in one country."

ALTERGLOBALISM AND THE INTERCONTINENTAL

Internationalism takes different forms today than it did forty years ago. Imperialist wars of intervention continue to occur at the beginning of the twenty-first century, raining bombs on innocents in the peripheral countries, and the necessity of a common fight against war and imperialist domination is still relevant. It is necessary to acknowledge all the limitations resulting from an authoritarian centralism present in movements such as the South Vietnamese NLF, the popular army of Giáp and Ho Chi Minh, and the liberation forces of the Portuguese colonies in Angola, Mozambique, and Guinea-Bissau. It is also necessary to acknowledge, unfortunately, that there are no similar forces of liberation with a program and emancipatory aims confronting the North American troops and their Atlantic allies in Afghanistan and Iraq today. Reactionary and oppressive movements such as the Taliban or al-Qaida obviously do not exert the same attraction as that of the third world revolutionaries of the 1960s and 1970s.

It is not by chance that the great internationalist event of 1967, the Tricontinental, was an assembly of revolutionary forces from the countries of Asia, Africa, and Latin America. Without being a "narrow third worldist," Guevara saw the dependent or colonial countries as the living center of the fight against imperialism and for a new society.

The new internationalism of the twenty-first century was opened with a meeting convened by the Zapatista Army of National Liberation in the mountains of Chiapas in 1996: the Intercontinental ("Intergalactic" in the ironic language of Subcomandante Marcos) Meeting for Humanity and Against Neoliberalism. It is no accident that it was a Guevarist revolutionary movement that convened this unforgettable meeting in which thousands of union members, peasant militants, indigenous people, intellectuals, students, and activists from different leftist currents participated. They came from forty countries across the world, including many from the United States and Europe. But the dynamic of the Intercontinental was different, more "universal," than that of the Tricontinental, with distinct methods of struggle, less centered on violence (without, for all that, being pacifist in orientation).

The movement for the global struggle against the brutal domination of neoliberal capitalism was born in the indigenous villages of Chiapas and experienced its baptism in the streets of Seattle in 1999, with the protests against the meeting of the World Trade Organzation (WTO). Che Guevara is, of all the great twentieth-century revolutionaries, probably the most popular within the alterglobalist movement.

This movement is undoubtedly the most significant anti-systemic resistance force at the beginning of the twenty-first century. This vast, loose conglomeration, a "movement of movements," takes visible form during the regional or world Social Forums and the large protest demonstrations against the WTO, the G-8, and the imperialist war in Iraq. A large decentralized network, it is many-sided, diverse, and heterogeneous, combining trade unions and peasant movements, NGOs and indigenous organizations, women's movements, and ecological organizations, intellectuals, and young activists. Far from being a weakness, its pluralism is one of the sources of the growing and expanding strength of the movement.

A new type of international solidarity is arising inside this vast network, somewhat different from that which characterized the internationalist mobilizations during the 1960s, Che's era.

Solidarity then appeared as support for liberation movements, particularly in the countries of the South, such as the Algerian, Cuban, and Vietnamese revolutions. This generous and fraternal tradition of solidarity with the oppressed has far from disappeared in the new movement for global justice that was formed in the 1990s. An obvious example is the immediate and spontaneous expression of sympathy and support for neo-Zapatismo following the uprising of the indigenous population of Chiapas on January 1, 1994. But in this context, something new appeared, a change in perspective: the participants in the 1996 intercontinental gathering came in solidarity with the Zapatistas, but they had a much larger objective, defined by the Zapatistas, to search for points of convergence in the struggle against a common enemy, neoliberalism, and to debate the possible alternatives for humanity.

This is, then, the new characteristic of the solidarities that are being forged within the movement of global resistance to capitalist globalization: the fight is defined as a function of immediate objectives, common to everyone (for example, to defeat the WTO), and there is a joint search for new paradigms of civilization. In other words, rather than a solidarity *with*, it is a solidarity *between* diverse organizations, social movements, and political forces from different countries and continents that help each other and join together in the same struggle to thwart the same global enemy.

To give an example: the international peasant network Via Campesina rallies movements as diverse as the French Peasant Confederation, Brazil's Landless Rural Workers' Movement, and large peasant movements from India. These organizations mutually support each other, exchange their experiences, and act jointly against neoliberal policies and their profiteers: the agribusiness multinationals, the seed monopolies, the manufacturers of genetically modified organisms, and large landowners. Their solidarity is reciprocal. Together they form one of the most powerful, active, and boisterous components of the global movement against capitalist globalization. Other examples could be given from the trade union, feminist (the World March of Women), ecological, or political realms of the movement.

The dynamics of the alterglobalist movement consist of three distinct and complementary moments: the negativity of resistance, concrete proposals, and the utopia of another world.

The first moment, the movement's point of departure, is the refusal, the protest, the imperative necessity of resisting the existing state of things. It is, in fact, the "international of resistance" that Jacques Derrida hoped and prayed for in his book *Specters of Marx*. The initial motivation of the crowds that mobilized in Seattle in 1999 was the wish actively to oppose, not "globalization" in itself, but its capitalist and liberal form, the *corporate globalization* with its succession of injustices and disasters:

growing inequalities between the North and the South, unemployment, social exclusion, environmental destruction, imperial wars, crimes against humanity. The movement was born, as we saw, with the cry of the Zapatistas in 1994: "*¡Ya basta!*" In the expression of this radical negativity, produced from a profound and irreducible indignation, lurks, in new forms, the Guevarist spirit of permanent rebellion. Extolling the dignity of indignation and the unconditional refusal of injustice, Daniel Bensaïd wrote: "The burning current of indignation is not soluble in the tepid waters of consensual resignation. . . . Indignation is a beginning, a way to get up and underway. You are indignant, you rise up and then you see."[12] The radical character of the movement comes, in large part, from this capacity for revolt and rebelliousness, this uncompromising disposition to say "No!" Critics of the movement and the conformist media have loudly insisted on the excessively "negative" character of the movement, its "purely" protest nature, and the absence of "realistic" alternative proposals. Such blackmail is not acceptable: even if the movement did not have a single proposal to make, its revolt would be *totally justified*. The street protests against the G-8 or against imperialist war are the concentrated, visible, and essential expression of this defiance towards the rules of the game imposed by the powerful. The movement is proud of its active negativity, its anti-establishment and rebellious fiber. Without this radical sentiment of refusal, the alterglobalist movement would not exist.

Against what opponent is this refusal directed? Is it the international financial institutions (WTO, IMF, World Bank)? Or is it neoliberal policies? Or even the large multinational monopolies? All these forces, responsible for the commodification of the world, are the targets of the movement. But focusing on commodification is more radical. The use of this word implies going to the root of the problem. What is the root of the totalitarian domination of the banks and monopolies, the dictatorship of the financial markets, and imperialist wars, if not the capitalist system itself? Certainly, not all parts of the alterglobalist movement are ready to draw this conclusion. Some still dream of a return to neo-Keynesianism, to the growth of the "glorious thirty years" following the end of the Second World War, or to a regulated capitalism "with a human face." These moderates have their place in the movement, but it is undeniable that a more radical tendency predominates. Most of the documents issued by the movement call into question not only neoliberal and warmongering policies, but also the *power of capital* itself. Take as an example the "Charter of Principles of the World Social Forum," drafted by the Brazilian Organization Committee (upon which sat not only labor unions and peasant movements, but also NGOs and a representative from the Catholic Church's Justice and Peace Commission) and approved, with several modifications, by the International Council of the World Social Forum. This document, one of the most representative and "consensual" of the alterglobalist movement, affirms: "The World Social Forum is an open meeting place for reflective thinking, democratic debate of ideas, formulation of proposals, free exchange of experiences, and interlinking for effective action, by groups and movements of civil society that are opposed to neo-liberalism and to domination of the world by capital and any form of imperialism, and are committed to building a planetary society directed towards fruitful relationships among Mankind and between it and the Earth. . . . The alternatives proposed at the World Social Forum stand in opposition to a process of globalization commanded by the large multinational corporations and by the governments and international institutions at the service of those corporations' interests, with the complicity of national governments."[13] The principal slogan of the movement, "the world is not a commodity," is not so far from the ideas of a certain Karl Marx, who wrote in the *1844 Manuscripts*: in the capitalist system "the worker becomes an ever cheaper commodity the more commodities he creates. The *devaluation* of the world of men is in direct proportion to the *increasing value* of the world of things."[14]

The radical character of the alterglobalist refusal undeniably challenges the capitalist nature of domination. Here, again, is an area where the ideas of the movement intersect those of the Argentine-Cuban revolutionary.

However, contrary to what the scribblers of the official consensus claim, the movement does not lack alternative proposals that are concrete, urgent, practical and immediately applicable. Certainly, no organization has approved a "common program" and no political force has laid down "its" plan. But, over the course of the forums and debates since Seattle and the First World Social Forum at Porto Alegre in January 2001, a group of demands have been outlined that, while not having unanimous support, are at least widely accepted and supported by the movement: the abolition of third world debt, taxation of financial transactions (inspired by the well-known Tobin tax), elimination of tax havens, a moratorium on GMOs (Genetically Modified Organisms), the right of people to food sovereignty, real equality between men and women, defense and extension of public services, the priority of health, education, and culture, and protection of the environment. These demands have been drawn up by alterglobalist international networks (the World March of Women, Attac, Focus on the Global South, Via Campesina, Committee for the Abolition of Third World Debt, etc.) and by various social movements and discussed in the Social Forums. One of the great qualities of the Forums has been to provide the possibility for a real confrontation and exchange of views between feminists and trade unionists, believers and non-believers, and militants from the North and from the South. In this process of confrontation and mutual enrichment, disagreements have not disappeared, but little by little the contours of a set of common proposals have emerged.

Are these proposals realistic? The question is wrong. In the existing balance of power, the elites and dominant classes refuse outright to consider them; they remain unimaginable for rigid, narrow-minded, and conformist neoliberal thought, they are intolerable for the representatives of capital, and, according to the social liberals, they are "unfortunately not feasible." But it is enough that the balance of power change and public opinion be mobilized for the leaders to be forced to back down and make concessions while striving to empty them of their substance. The important thing about these proposals is that they are extendable: any partial victory, any conquest, any advance makes it possible to move on to the next step, the higher step, to a more radical demand. This is something different from what is found in the traditional workers' movement. It is a transitional dynamic that leads, in the end, to calling the system itself into question.

We now come to the third moment, as important as the preceding ones: the utopian dimension of the movement. It also is radical: "Another world is possible." It is not a question of simply correcting the excesses of the capitalist world and its horrendous neoliberal policies, but of dreaming and fighting for *another civilization*, another economic and social paradigm, and another form of living together on the planet. Measured against this ambition, it is right to recover the ethical, revolutionary, and humanist heritage of Guevara. The alterglobalist utopia appears, above all, in the sharing of certain *common values*, which alone outline the contours of this other "possible world," one that is profoundly human.

The first of these values is centered on the human being. The utopia of the movement remains resolutely humanist; it demands that the needs and aspirations of human beings become the vital center of a reorganization of the economy and society. It is a revolt against the commodification of men and women and their relationships, against the transformation of love, culture, life, and health into marketable goods, and against the trade of bodies, organs, and persons. Today, this revolt is more relevant than ever because the neoliberal doctrine sees everything as an opportunity for competition, valorization, and marketing. It is urgently necessary to think of another social model, far from absolute reification and fetishism. It is no accident that the movement speaks to all humans, even if it privileges the oppressed and exploited as actors of social change. Defense of the environment is inspired by humanism: preserving ecological balances, preventing the disaster of climate change, and protecting nature against the terrible destruction of capitalist productivism are the necessary conditions for ensuring the continuity of human life on the planet.

Democracy is another essential value of the alterglobalist utopia. today attacked by the domination of capitalist finance. The idea that participatory democracy is a superior form for the exercise of citizenship, as it overcomes many of the limitations of traditional representative systems by allowing the population to directly exercise the power of decision making and control, is one of the central themes of the movement. This is a utopian value insofar as it calls into question existing forms of power, but at the same time it is already practiced, in an experimental form, in numerous cities. The great challenge from the point of view of a project for an alternative society is to extend democracy to the economic and social terrain. Why allow the exclusive power of an elite in this area when it is refused in the political sphere? It remains to apply these democratic principles to the movement itself and to the World Social Forums, a process that is still trying to find its way and is riddled with contradictions.

Capital has replaced the three great revolutionary values of the past—liberty, equality, and fraternity—with more "modern" concepts: liberalism, equity, and charity. The alterglobalist utopia takes as its own the values of 1789, but gives them a new significance. Liberty is not only freedom of expression, organization, thought, criticism, and assembly, conquered with difficulty through centuries of struggle against absolutism, fascism, and dictatorships. It is also, and today more than ever, liberty in relation to another form of absolutism: the dictatorship of financial markets and of the elite of bankers and leaders of multinational corporations who impose their interests on the whole planet. As for equality, it involves not only the gap between the affluent and the deprived, but also the inequality between nations, ethnic groups, and men and women. Finally, the notion of fraternity is enhanced and developed by being replaced with the value of solidarity. That is, by relations of cooperation, sharing, and mutual aid. The expression "civilization of solidarity" is a good summary of the movement's alternative project. It implies not only a radically different economic and political structure, but also an alternative society that celebrates the ideas of the common good, the general interest, universal rights, and selflessness.

Another important value of alterglobalism is diversity. The new world the movement dreams of is not a homogeneous universe, where everyone must imitate a single model. We want, as the Zapatistas say, "one world with many worlds in it." A plurality of languages, cultures, musical traditions, foods, and forms of life is an immense wealth that should be cultivated.

These values do not define a paradigm of society for the future. They provide paths to follow, openings. The road toward utopia is not completely mapped out. Those who walk that road will map it themselves.

For many of the participants in the forums and demonstrations, socialism is the name of this utopia. It is a hope shared by Marxists and libertarians, Christians and left ecologists, as well as by a significant number of trade union militants, peasants, feminists, and indigenous people. A socialist democracy means that, as Guevara proposed in his *Critical Notes on Political Economy*, the important socioeconomic choices, priorities in matters of investments, and the fundamental direction of production and distribution are democratically discussed and decided by the population and not by a handful of exploiters according to supposed "laws of the market" (or even, an already failed variation, by an all-powerful politburo).

Socialism must truly be a total democracy through which the people govern themselves, by and for themselves, in political and social equality. In other words, a society without classes that guarantees to each person the individual freedom to be able to enjoy a new type of liberty, freed from the yoke of economic exploitation as well as political and hierarchical constraints. In brief, a world able to fulfill the Marxist slogan: "From each according to her ability, to each according to her needs."

A few paths exist to reach this goal. By generalizing the principle of free access, which only partially exists in the benefits from certain public services, society can restrict the role of money to its simplest expression: in short, pocket money. In order to be protected from the demands of the market and fight against the resulting waste, the population can program, that is, plan the manufacture of goods and services to satisfy the well-being of each person and meet real needs. The people themselves are the best placed to estimate their own needs and best know what should be produced and how it should be produced. Residents of neighborhoods are better able than anyone else to know what type of housing, transportation, garbage collection, and public spaces they need. The inhabitants of cities are in a position to know the number of schools, hospitals or businesses that are necessary. And in their workplaces the workers can, without being interfered with by any hierarchy, satisfy orders for goods or services coming from the society. First at the level of a region or a country, then at the level of a continent or the planet, it is the population itself that controls the wealth. It can make decisions, through democratic planning, about the priorities in production and consumption, investments in new industries (renewable energy, for example), and the abandonment of old production methods (nuclear energy, for example).

This socialist self-management is the most democratic form of society. Although he was aware of this, Guevara opposed self-management in a context where the decentralization of business enterprises goes hand in hand with the financial autonomy of production units, an arrangement that, he believed, would inevitably lead to competition. He rightly fought against all residues and all pockets of the market economy. Self-management fundamentally poses the question of the ownership of the large means of production with which a system is equipped, because at this level ownership is power. Who decides? A sound democracy is one that makes it possible to decide on all public choices, including economic ones, within democratically elected assemblies. From this perspective, the kind of planning Che was in favor of is not in opposition to self-management. Socialism, if it is not just fine words, cannot be summed up simply as a government that changes hands. The state is not neutral. To establish new institutions that function from the bottom up and not the top down, it is necessary to get rid of the old state structure and create mechanisms of democratic control. Guevara had arrived at the conclusion, through his own experience, that it was impossible to change society without social change. This type of change ultimately implies the replacement of the state by non-state forms of power, founded on direct popular participation, such as councils and assemblies.

In the debate on twenty-first-century socialism, which is developing with increasing energy not only in Venezuela but throughout Latin America and beyond, the heritage of Che's humanist and revolutionary Marxism is one of the important moral and political reference points. The quest for a restored socialism is not the dream of an unwavering handful. Its utopianism lies in its effort to envisage the future in order to try to imagine, today, what an alternative to capitalism could look like. But it also remains a real movement, continually gestating within today's society, which does away with the existing order on the basis of its own contradictions. Capitalism generates exploitation, inequalities, and wars and thus also gives rise to human revolts. In its development, it creates the potential social conditions for its own overturning. For example, today, across the planet, the number of exploited, those who sell their manual or intellectual labor-power in order to survive, has never been so large. An "immense number that has never realized its power," as the communard Louise Michel put it.[15] The paradox of the contemporary lies in this contradiction: never has this new wage-earning class been so large, but never has its consciousness of itself as a class been so repressed. "Divide and conquer" is the maxim of the owning classes. Guevara proposed to fight it through a wider popular unity for resistance and for building a new society. He worked at the divide between workers and peasants in order to transcend the social discord that weighed so heavily on the struggles of his time.

Forty years later, new divisions have emerged within populations. By way of growing job insecurity and the increasing privatization of public space, neoliberalism has considerably reduced pockets of solidarity. Within popular strata, invisible walls have been built from above. The border guards are prejudices: between the unemployed and employed, the insecure and the entitled, men and women, young and old, citizens and immigrants.

Despite everything, these new wage-earning strata are learning to resist capitalist globalization together. Within the renewal of international struggles many foundational experiences are emerging that make it possible to believe in the elaboration of a credible social project. Socialism and communism in the nineteenth century were born from the dialectic between thinking (the thinking of Fourier, Marx, Engels, Bakunin, and many others) and experience gained from the struggle of organizations of the oppressed. It is from below that hope came. It is from below that it will be reborn. A new political era is approaching. The revolutionaries of today are tackling it with their share of legitimate doubt, but also with deeply held convictions. The red and the black of Guevara's flag resist, better than other colors, the disruptions underway and the dominant spirit of the times. For Che, socialism was not a "turnkey" social project. The fight to overturn capitalism has to be experienced by each individual as a personal urgency, an urgency that today is more relevant than ever.

Appendix

Che: A Thinker of Acts

by Daniel Bensaïd

The following transcript is a speech given at a meeting on Che Guevara in July 1997 at an international youth camp.

This event is devoted to paying homage to Che Guevara, militant revolutionary, on the eve of the thirtieth anniversary of his death. At this moment, a series of books and films have appeared that are reopening the debate on his personality and his role in the history of the oppressed.

For some, he is the very image of the fanatic driven by despair, compelled into a suicidal headlong flight, searching for his own death, who unfortunately involved naive or shortsighted men and women in his personal adventure.

For others, he is an immaculate religious image, the incarnation of a Christ-like perfection. Tomorrow, perhaps, they will seek to build a mausoleum to hold his recovered remains and celebrate him in a cult that represents just the opposite of his own view of the world and humanity.

For us, who want neither gods nor masters, nor idols, what interests us in the figure of Che, in his meteoric passage through contemporary history, is, on the contrary, the quite simply human character of the militant, with his strengths and weaknesses, whose life and actions encapsulate the great hopes and great disillusions of this century that is now coming to an end.

I will start from the interest that this person always provokes in the opinion of generations of people who have no direct knowledge of his struggles. This is quite different from many others who were famous. Che's life is a sort of concentrated, compressed summary of the century's revolutionary experience. With him, around him, everything moved very quickly. Born in 1928, he died in 1967, at age 39. His active political life lasted less than fifteen years. It was, however, more than full: in 1954, he participated in the Guatemalan resistance to imperialist intervention; from 1956 to 1959, he was a Cuban guerilla, from the landing of the *Granma* to the victorious entry into Havana; from 1959 to 1965, he carried out governmental responsibilities and diplomatic missions; in 1966, he participated in fighting in the Congo; in 1967, he fought and died in Bolivia. Fifteen extraordinarily active years: like a Saint-Just, Che lived a hurried life, more intensely than most who had longer lives.

It is not only this brevity that is striking, but also the accelerated trajectory of his experience in the century. His first motorcycle journey through Latin America was an initiation to reality, the imperialist domination of the continent, and the resulting misery, poverty, and cultural dependence. That experience forged in him a profoundly rebellious, anti-imperialist conviction, which was the first motivation of his commitment.

Then, through the experience of the Cuban revolution, he observed that an anti-dictatorial, national liberation struggle, just a stone's throw from the imperialist power, would not be able to reach its objectives by remaining shackled to agreements with corrupt, dependent, and weak national bourgeoisies. He concluded that the only solution for real independence lies in the struggle for socialism. Here lies the origin of his famous formula: "Either socialist revolution or caricature of revolution," which returns, in its own way, to the terms and content of the opposition between "socialism in one country" and permanent revolution. While some of our generation, who already long knew that, recognized in Che a comrade and brother in arms, many also rediscovered Trotskyism from Guevarism.

Finally, his third great experience as minister in the revolutionary government was one characterized by conflictual relationships with the "brother countries" of the socialist camp. In negotiating support and economic and military cooperation, and in debating international politics with Chinese and Soviet leaders, Che came to a terrible conclusion that he had the courage—you have to imagine the era and the context in order to assess his audacity—to express publicly in a speech that has remained famous, delivered in Algiers in 1965 after a trip to the Soviet Union and China. It was a challenge and a veritable indictment of the absence of internationalism in the policy of the so-called socialist states. He reproaches them, first of all, with applying conditions of trade to the poorest countries typical of the world market dominated by imperialism. He also explicitly reproaches them with not providing unconditional aid, including military aid, to the liberation struggles in the Congo and, particularly, Vietnam.

The Algiers speech is a strong accusation against the lack of international solidarity on the part of these so-called socialist countries. Thus, it was not by chance that, after his return from Algiers, Che no longer appeared in public in Cuba. It now appears, according to all the available documents and witnesses, that the Soviet leadership had clearly told the Cuban leadership that he had become undesirable, that he could no longer represent the Cuban revolution in any capacity, and that it was necessary to eliminate him or find him another job. This is one of the reasons, not the only, of course, that helps us to understand the last years of Che's life, his presence in the Congo in 1966 and his Bolivian expedition the following year.

This hurried trajectory through the tragedy of the century leads us to a question much discussed today, including on the revolutionary Left, in which Che's actions are sometimes presented as romantic and suicidal madness, perhaps well intentioned but irrelevant to reality. Beyond his personal psychological characteristics (we all have a shadow side, our childhood traumas and bizarre compulsions), Che's choices and behavior result from a particularly acute political awareness of what was then at stake, from a completely lucid understanding of the reality of the international situation, characterized by the partnership in conflict of the great powers, and the historical ordeal of the imperialist escalation in Vietnam. His decisions were political. They demonstrate a perfect, albeit unusual—even among revolutionaries—agreement between thought and action.

One can say of him what Dionys Mascolo could write about Saint-Just: he was "a thinker of acts."

What he wrote in his last texts, particularly in his famous 1967 message to the Tricontinental, from which many of you should at least be able to read extracts, are simple, almost banal, things. But for a number of people who claimed to be revolutionaries, who considered themselves to be guardians of the revolutionary heritage, but without acting on that heritage, these words resonated like a ruthless challenge. You know these small phrases.

"The duty of any revolutionary is to make the revolution." Obviously. Of course. But this is a way of denouncing, in the context, all the so-called revolutionaries who not only did not seek to make the revolution, who managed secure incomes, but who torpedoed the efforts of people to liberate themselves.

"Socialist revolution or caricature of revolution": a new society and new human beings are not built with the same morals, same methods, same relations of power, the same conception of labor as in the old world. All aspects of social relations, including those of everyday life, personal relations, and gender relations, must be changed completely. In a very important text, *Socialism and Man in Cuba*, Che criticizes the official literature and philosophy of the so-called socialist countries by calling for the renewal of thought, for leaving dogmas behind, for a rupture with the heavy culture of state and party orthodoxies.

The weight of the bureaucratic edifice was so heavy to dislodge, it required such energy, such effort, that the rupture certainly was not going to happen without risks. Some have reproached Che with voluntarism—in other words, an excessive will that escapes from reality—or "leftism." Unfortunately, he himself was perfectly aware, in his last struggles, of the contradictions in the situation, of an almost desperate race against time with barbarism. In his message to the Tricontinental, he spoke of "the tragic solitude of the Vietnamese people" in their struggle against American intervention. This tragic solitude was also his own solitude in Bolivia. It is the result, he said, "of an illogical moment in the history of humanity." Illogical because, at the moment when people are rising up and shaking off the yoke of oppression, those who should come to their aid, without selling their support, are lacking and even put spokes in the wheels.

Finally, Che's deeply moving course in Bolivia, which is captured quite poignantly in Dindo's film,[1] and which could appear as a senseless endeavor in a region itself desolate and almost deserted, results from an implacable logic in an illogical world. Che: a revolutionary through logic! Prohibited from returning to Cuba after his speech in Algiers, he had attempted to open a new stage of the African revolution in the Congo after independence and the assassination of Patrice Lumumba in 1961. The failure was bitter. He remained, despite everything, profoundly convinced that, if it remained isolated in the world, within reach of the American coast, the Cuban revolution would only be subjected, little by little, to the conditions and commands of the "brother countries," falling under their bureaucratic rule. The imperative, the revolutionary duty—whether it succeed or not—was from that point on to do everything to break the circle, smash the siege, to extend the revolution beginning with the closest place, the continent he knew well from his travels. The project was undoubtedly too ambitious, enormous, but it was not without political sense. It was not a question of taking power in Bolivia, but of assembling and training several hundred combatants from at least five countries so as to make Bolivia into the starting point, the continental center for continental subversion.

On issuing the slogan "Create two, three, many Vietnams," Che added that many would die, "victims of their errors." He himself had committed such errors and not the least. For a start, he underestimated the extent of the sabotage aimed at him by the Soviet leadership and the official Bolivian communist leaders. According to his comrade in arms in Bolivia, Colonel Dariel Alarcon ("Benigno"), after his meeting with the Secretary-General of the party, Mario Monje, he gathered the handful of Cubans engaged at his side to explain to them that the conditions were not those that had initially been anticipated, that this would be very hard, maybe hopeless, that they could, consequently, feel free to leave without shame, which no one did. Driven into a political and historical impasse, his struggle could still have meaning, it could be a message, a heritage to transmit, that we, in return, have the responsibility of inheriting, of making come alive and transmitting in turn.

Like all human beings, Che has his differences, limitations, and faults. No one, or almost no one, contests certain notable personality traits: an intransigent sense of justice, an egalitarian hate of privilege, an obstinate courage. These qualities are accompanied by a toughness, because a fight to the death against a powerful, unscrupulous enemy is not a gala dinner. Also because, being ill, he imposed on others a toughness that he imposed on himself. Circumstances and behaviors can always be discussed.

As far as we are concerned, it is important above all to note the political limitations of his experience, without reducing their contribution. He was educated in the quite particular circumstances of the Cuban revolution, itself a short historical period: less than three years between the landing of the *Granma* and the victorious entry into Havana, between the initial skirmishes of a handful of shipwreck survivors and the victory of the rebel army. Often, the legend of the Cuban Revolution, maintained by its own actors, is confined to a mythical story and a simplified epic, leaving the antecedents in the shadows, the existence of a social, agrarian, and urban movement, the role of the networks, the multiplicity of protagonists, as if the Cuban Revolution was reduced to the triumphal march of Fidel and his followers. The fact remains that the actors themselves were able to convince themselves of the truth of their own legend to the point of according, under the pressure of the urgency, excessive value to the exemplary action, to vanguardist audacity. Marching in front, showing the way, making sacrifices makes it possible to go into combat, to take improbable positions, and galvanize energies during a campaign. But the method has its limits when it is a question of building something in the long term, transforming the economy, and revolutionizing the culture. For that, the collective intelligence and energy of the organized multitude are necessary, and the assimilation of a pluralist and democratic culture is required for the resolution of contradictions. Patience and tenacity are also necessary.

Che was the classic example of a man in a hurry. He rushed through the world with the feeling, justifiable enough, that the great disasters of the century were always on his heels. His individual dedication, in work and in combat, his personal frugality and asceticism in the face of privilege, could not replace institutions, rules, collective experience, for which the military style of the guerilla is no longer sufficient. Saint-Just had this intuition himself, when, noting that the revolution was frozen, he envisaged, just before mounting the scaffold, the necessity of republican institutions.

This weakness is understandable. In the 1960s, the Latin American revolutionary movement was dominated by the prospect of war. The war in Vietnam, certainly, embedded as it was in the unstable equilibrium of the Cold War (illustrated by the Cuban missile crisis). And the recent Algerian war for independence. In war, the opposition between allies and enemies does not easily accommodate nuances. Relations of authority and command are inevitable, which provide simple and rapid responses to complex questions. This efficiency is appropriate, but it has its limits. It is on these limits that we should today focus our critical analysis of Che without in the least diminishing the world that we owe to him.

I have insisted at length on the importance of such a person for a generation—my generation—which already, alas, has several decades of militant activity behind it. It is important now to go back over the relevance of the heritage, if we want to make something useful and living out of it and not a sad object for worship and commemoration. It is necessary to understand why his presence is still so active, in Latin America and throughout the world.

On the one hand, because, after the other great Latin American revolutionary figures, such as the Cuban Julio Antonio Mella or the Peruyian José Carlos Mariatégui, Che provided an example of a non-Stalinist revolutionary, resolutely internationalist, and anti-bureaucratic. From this perspective, the Zapatista movement in Mexico carries on something of this tradition. There is something of Che's spirit in the improbable audacity of the uprising on January 1, 1994, in San Critobal de las Casas, following the disintegration of the USSR, the Gulf War, in the midst of the liberal planetary offensive, at the time of the free trade treaty with the United States signed by Mexico (NAFTA). In these conditions, to raise the flag of revolt appears to go against the tide of the time, to go the wrong way against the fate proclaimed by History. It is, however, an act of resistance and a challenge to the way things are, just like Che.

While this continuity is important, many other experiences have been accumulated over the last thirty years in Latin America: the Popular Unity government and the dictatorship in Chile, military *coups d'état* in Uruguay and Argentina, the Colombian guerillas, wars in Central America, and the birth of a union movement and mass workers' party in Brazil. All of that contributes to the formation of a new political culture, more democratic, more pluralist, more attached to the autonomy of social, union, and agrarian organizations. The twist made by Zapatista irony, the apology that Marcos makes for a "heroism of life," testifies, in its own way, to these changes: "We do not want," writes Subcomandante Marcos, "that anyone should inherit the cult of death from us. We want to leave behind the cult of struggle. And, as is said here, in order to fight, it is necessary to be alive; dead, it is not possible to fight. Truly, a good part of our military training aimed at not dying: 'The first duty of a combatant is to not die,' we said to them." That does not prevent them from risking their lives over and over.

Che's image in the world remains above all that of an internationalist in his acts, implacably opposed to a world abandoned to the plundering and miseries of imperial globalization. This accounts for his relevance and influence. In this cynical and literally demoralized world, it proves that agreement between morality and politics is possible, that politics is not inevitably immoral and morality inevitably apolitical, that it is possible to hold onto both ends. His prestige in the eyes of youth also comes from the fact that he represents the perhaps unique case of a revolutionary who, having attained power, was capable of leaving it in order to commit his strength to a struggle that cannot end in a single country. If he interests you and attracts you still today, it is for all these reasons and also because, having died at thirty-nine years of age, still young, his image inextricably links together youth and revolution.

Concerning Ernesto Che Guevara

by Subcomandante Marcos
Spokesperson for the Zapatista Army of National Liberation (EZLN)[1]

Forty years ago, in 1966, after having been "nowhere,"[2] a man prepared memory and hope so that life could return to America. Ramon was his *nom de guerre*. In one of the numerous hidden recesses of American Reality, this man remembered, and in his memories every man and woman who lived and offered their lives for America lived again. His name and his memory were buried by the eternal gravediggers of history. According to some, his first name was Ernesto and his last name was Guevara de la Serna. For us, he was and remains *Che*.

At Punta del Este, he denounced the politics of power that, from the offices of the World Bank, suggested building latrines as a solution to the serious poverty of the countries of America. Since then, poverty in America has grown in the same proportion as its wealth has been pillaged by the ever wealthy. The "latrinocracy" has also changed, but only in name. In one of the countries of America, it assumes the paradoxical name "Solidarity." However, despite the lexical mirages, the basic operation of the "latrinocracy" is still the same: today as yesterday, the poor are at the bottom of the latrines and the wealthy sit on the toilet seat.

Che's critique of power did not involve accepting the shortcomings of or justifying a particular system. Condemning the fact that many people are opposed to existing power arrangements on the basis of principles that are similar to those used to justify those arrangements, but just hidden under a different name, he wrote in 1964: "I am the last person in the world to claim to have finished with the subject or have decreed some type of papal benediction on these contradictions and others. Unfortunately, in the eyes of most people, and even in mine, praising a system has more effect than its scientific analysis."

Citizen of the world, Che reminds us of what we have known since Spartacus, and sometimes forget: in the struggle against injustices, humanity finds a course that teaches it, makes it better, and more human.

A little later, memory and hope held his pen so that he could write in his farewell letter: "One day they came by and asked who should be notified in case of death, and the real possibility of that fact struck us all. Later we knew that it was true, that in a revolution one wins or dies (if it is a real one). . . . Other nations of the world call for my modest efforts." And that is the way that Che followed his path.

To say "adieu," to say "see you later," Che said, "until victory, forever," as if to say "we'll see each other soon."

Forty years after, in the early hours of the day when the moon recovers bits of light torn from it by the monthly bite of time, and when a comet disguised as a street lamp needlessly watches over the doors of night, I looked for a text to support the initial words of this reflection.

I re-read everything, from Pablo Neruda to Julio Cortázar, from Walt Whitman to Juan Rulfo. A waste of time; constantly, Che's image, with his dreamy eyes, in the school at La Higuera,[3] claimed its place between my hands. From Bolivia, his half-closed eyes and ironic smile, which recounted what happened and promised what was going to happen, had reached us.

I said "dreamy"? Perhaps I should have said "dead." For some, he is dead, for others, he is just sleeping. Who is wrong? Forty years ago, Che prepared the transformation of American reality and power prepared his destruction. Forty years ago, power claimed that the end of history had occurred in the El Yuro[4] ravine. It claimed that the possibility of a better world, a different world, had been destroyed once and for all. It maintained that the time of rebellions was over.

Chronology of Important Dates

June 14, 1928. Ernesto Guevara Lynch de la Serna, son of Celia de la Serna and Ernesto Guevara Lynch, born at Rosario de Santa Fé, Argentina.

1935. With a serious case of asthma, Ernesto cannot follow the usual schooling. His mother takes charge of his education. He quite quickly develops a passion for sports.

1937. Ernesto's father establishes a committee of support for the Spanish Republic.

1945–1951. Ernesto enrolls in medical school. He works as a nurse on a tanker, then as a practitioner in a municipal health center. This is the period in Argentina of the populist government of General Juan Domingo Perón.

December 1951. Beginning of the motorcycle trip with Alberto Granado. They cross Argentina, Chile, Peru, Colombia, and reach Venezuela in July 1952.

November 1952. Upon returning to Buenos Aires, Ernesto Guevara obtains his medical degree.

July 1953. He sets off again on a second trip in Latin America with his friend Carlos Ferrer. Travels through Bolivia, where the Paz Estenssoro government is implementing some social reforms. Guevara stays in Ecuador and reaches Guatemala, where the democratic government of Colonel Arbenz is attempting to resist the large American companies. He meets Hilda Gadea Acosta there, an exiled Peruvian, who is going to become his first wife. He becomes involved with a group of Cuban refugees who just arrived in Guatemala after the failure of the assault on the Moncada Barracks. He writes to his mother: "In Guatemala, I could become very rich by devoting myself to the study of allergies. But this would be to betray in the most horrible way these two 'I's' that I carry, my socialist 'I' and my traveler 'I'." He leaves Guatemala after the overthrow, without resistance, of the Arbenz government by mercenaries in the service of the CIA, led by Castillo Armas.

September 1954. Settled in Mexico, Guevara finds work in several hospitals.

July–August 1955. He is introduced to Fidel Castro. After a night of intense conversation, Castro recruits him as doctor for the revolutionary expedition that he is preparing against the Batista dictatorship in Cuba.

March 1956. Birth of his daughter Hildita.

June 1956. Participates in military training for Cuban militants, led by General Alvarez Bayo, a former officer of the Spanish Republican Army, exiled in Mexico. He is imprisoned for more than a month with his exiled Cuban friends. It is the latter who give him the nickname "Che," an untranslatable expression often used in conversation by Argentines.

November 1956. The ship *Granma* leaves Mexico for Cuba. Its eighty-two passengers aim at overthrowing the Batista regime and organizing a revolution on the island. They land on December 2, already spotted by the enemy. The guerilla group reforms in the mountains on December 21. On January 17, attack on a barracks and first victory.

May–June 1957. The group is strengthened and finds weapons. Guevara operates in the Sierra Maestra, in the north of the island, with his Fourth Column. Batista launches a massive operation against it.

August 1958. Che's column has 148 men. With the aim of cutting the island in half, his column carries out a march of forty-six days.

December 30, 1958. Comandante Guevara wins the decisive battle of Santa Clara. He is wounded in the left arm. General uprising in Cuba. Batista flees.

January 2, 1959. Che and Camilo Cienfuegos enter Havana, Castro enters Santiago de Cuba.

June 2, 1959. He marries Aleida March, a guerilla companion. He travels as ambassador to African and Asian countries to stabilize Cuba's economic relations with these countries. Upon his return, he is named manager of industrialization for the National Institute of Agrarian Reform, then president of the National Bank.

October 1960. He travels in the USSR, Czechoslovakia, the German Democratic Republic, China, and North Korea.

February 1961. As Minister of Industry, Che writes: "If communism was not intended to lead to the creation of a new man, it would have no meaning."

April 1961. Landing at Playa Girón, the Bay of Pigs, of 1500 counterrevolutionaries supported by the United States, quickly defeated and captured.

August 1961. Che delivers an anti-imperialist speech at Punta del Este (Uruguay) during a conference of Latin American governments.

October 1962. Missile crisis between the United States and the USSR (the latter stationed missiles in Cuba). Che Guevara is charged with organizing the defense of the western front in case of a North American invasion.

July 1963. He visits Ben Bella's Algeria.

1963–1964. He begins an important debate on the Cuban economic model, the law of value, and planning, in which Cuban economists participate, as well as Charles Bettelheim, a French economist who is then advising the governments of several recently decolonized countries. The latter is opposed to Che's theses, while Ernest Mandel, Belgian Marxist economist and leader of the Unified Secretariat of the Fourth International (Trotskyist), supports them.

March–April 1964. He leads the Cuban delegation to the United Nations Conference on Trade and Development in Geneva.

December 9, 1964. Speech in favor of the liberation of Latin America at the United Nations General Assembly in New York.

January–March 1965. He travels in Africa. He visits Mali, Congo-Brazzaville, Ghana, and Tanzania.

February 1965. Speech in Algiers to the "Second Economic Seminar on Afro-Asian Solidarity" in which he formulates a caustic critique of the complicity of the "socialist" countries with the practice of unequal exchange in the system of world trade.

March 1965. Return to Cuba. Guevara's last public appearance with the Cuban leadership. Leaves for Africa, where he participates in combat with the Lumumbist forces against the neocolonial regime in the Congo. Defeat of his attempt. Publication of the pamphlet *Socialism and Man in Cuba*.

October 3, 1965. Castro publicly reads Che's farewell message: "Other nations of the world summon my modest efforts."

1966. Stays in Tanzania, then in Prague. He completes some notebooks, including what will later be published as *Critical Notes on Political Economy*, a critical commentary on the *Manual of Political Economy* of the Academy of Sciences of the USSR.

November 3, 1966. Che leaves for Bolivia to lead a revolutionary guerilla campaign.

November 6, 1966. He joins the base of the Bolivian guerilla group at Ñancahuazú.

April 1967. Publication of his "Message to the Tricontinental Conference," which is being held in Havana.

June-October 1967. The Bolivian military dictatorship, supported by the United States, deploys large military forces against Che and his small group of guerillas. After several initial victories, Che's fighting forces, the ELN (*Ejército Liberación Nacional*—National Liberation Army), are gradually decimated.

October 8, 1967. Last battle at Quebrada del Yuro. Wounded, his arm broken, Che is taken prisoner along with several of his comrades. He does not respond to any questions while under interrogation. He is led to the village of La Higuera and imprisoned in a school classroom under strong guard.

October 9, 1967. He is executed by submachine gun fire by order of Bolivian President Barrientos and the CIA.

Notes

1. A MARXIST HUMANISM

1. Paco Ignacio Taibo II, *Guevara, Also Known as Che*, trans. Martin Michael Roberts (New York: St. Martin's Press, 1997), 298. [Translation modified. Trans.]
2. Ernesto Che Guevara, "Honoring José Marti," in *Che: Selected Works of Ernesto Guevara*, ed. Rolando E. Bonachea and Nelson P. Valdes (Cambridge, MA: MIT Press, 1969), 211.
3. Guevara, "Lettre à María Rosario Guevara," in *Oeuvres III, Textes politiques* (Paris: Maspero, 1971), 316.
4. Guevara, "What a Young Communist Should Be," in *Che Guevara and the Cuban Revolution: Writings and Speeches of Ernesto Che Guevara*, ed. David Deutschmann (Sydney: Pathfinder/Pacific and Asia, 1987), 184.
5. Guevara, *The Motorcycle Diaries: Notes on a Latin American Journey* (New York: Ocean Press, 2003), 32.
6. Guevara, "Development of a Marxist Revolution," July 28, 1960, in *Che: Selected Works of Ernesto Guevara*, 247.
7. Guevara, "Un péché dans la révolution," February 12, 1962.
8. Guevara, "On the Budgetary System of Finance," in *Che: Selected Works of Ernesto Guevara*, 113.
9. Ibid.
10. Guevara, "Socialist Planning," in *Venceremos! The Speeches and Writings of Che Guevara*, ed. John Gerassi (New York: Simon and Schuster, 1968), 406.
11. Ibid., 113.
12. Within the context of the international communist movement, the term "leftist" has been pejorative since it was first popularized by Lenin's 1920 work, *Left-Wing Communism: An Infantile Disorder*, as an attempt to denounce sectarian

attitudes in the workers' movement. In the Stalinist and post-Stalinist eras, this term serves to discredit tendencies of the workers' movement that contested the direction of the Communist Party. The term was in vogue at the end of the 1960s, when the "orthodox" line was increasingly contested throughout the whole world.

13. Guevara, "Cuba: Exceptional Case or Vanguard in the Struggle against Colonialism?" in *Che: Selected Works of Ernesto Guevara*, 70.
14. Guevara, "Socialism and Man in Cuba," ibid., 156.
15. Ibid., 158, 162.
16. Ibid., 155.
17. Guevara, "What a Young Communist Should Be," in *Che Guevara and the Cuban Revolution: Writings and Speeches of Ernesto Che Guevara*, 177.
18. Guevara, "Socialism and Man in Cuba," ibid., 169.
19. Guevara, "What a Young Communist Should Be," ibid., 179.
20. Ibid., 183.
21. Ibid., 184.
22. Guevara, "Message to the Tricontinental," in *Che Guevara and the Cuban Revolution: Writings and Speeches of Ernesto Che Guevara*, 172.
23. Guevara, "Socialism and Man in Cuba," in *Che Guevara and the Cuban Revolution: Writings and Speeches of Ernesto Che Guevara*, 161.
24. Ibid., 159.
25. Guevara, "The Cadre, Backbone of the Revolution," ibid., 74.
26. Guevara, "Socialism and Man in Cuba," ibid.,167.
27. Guevara, "Message to the Tricontinental," ibid., 180.
28. Guevara, *The Diary of Che Guevara* (New York: Bantam Books, 1968), 131.
29. Ibid., 122.
30. Frantz Fanon, *The Wretched of the Earth* (New York: Grove Press, 1968), 93–94.
31. Louise Michel, *Mémoires* (Paris: Maspero, 1976), 345–346.
32. Guevara. *Apuntes críticos a la Economía Política* (Melbourne, Australia: Ocean Press 2006). English edition to be published as *Critical Notes on Political Economy: A Revolutionary Humanist Approach to Marxist Economics* (Melbourne, Australia: Ocean Press, 2008).
33. Guevara, "What a Young Communist Should Be," in *Che Guevara and the Cuban Revolution: Writings and Speeches of Ernesto Che Guevara*, 181.
34. Louise Michel, *Mémoires,* 228.
35. Guevara, "Une faute de la revolution," in *Oeuvres*, v. 5, 16–20.
36. Auguste Blanqui, "Discours à la Société des Amis du Peuple," February 2, 1832, in *Auguste Blanqui, Textes choisis* (Paris: Editions sociales, 1971), 93.
37. Guevara, *Guerrilla Warfare* (Lincoln: University of Nebraska Press, 1985), 131.
38. Ibid., 65.
39. Guevara, *Diary of Che Guevara*, 154.
40. Guevara, "Sur la construction du Parti," in *Oeuvres III, Textes politique,*(Paris:

Maspero, 1971), 140.
41. Guevara, "Tactics and Strategy of the Latin American Revolution," in *Che: Selected Works of Ernesto Guevara*, 83.
42. Guevara, "Socialism and Man in Cuba," ibid., 157.
43. Ibid., 158.
44. Ibid., 157.
45. Ibid., 162.
46. Ibid.
47. Ibid., 167.
48. Antonio Gramsci, *Selections from the Prison Notebooks of Antonio Gramsci*, ed. and trans. Quintin Hoare and Geoffrey Nowell Smith (New York: International Publishers, 1971), 361.

2. SOCIALIST REVOLUTION OR CARICATURE OF REVOLUTION?

1. Guevara, "Tactics and Strategy of the Latin American Revolution," in *Che: Selected Works of Ernesto Guevara*, 87.
2. Guevara,"Political Sovereignty and Economic Independence," ibid., 221.
3. Ibid. 217.
4. Andrew Sinclair, *Che Guevara* (New York: Viking, 1970), 1.
5. Government troops who suppressed the Commune. –Trans.
6. Guevara, "Tactics and Strategy of the Latin American Revolution," in *Che: Selected Works of Ernesto Guevara*, 80.
7. Guevara, *Guerrilla Warfare*, 48.
8. Guevara, "Tactics and Strategy of the Latin American Revolution," in *Che: Selected Works of Ernesto Guevara*, 78.
9. Guevara, "Cuba: Exceptional Case or Vanguard in the Struggle against Colonialism?," ibid., 66.
10. Guevara, "Guerrilla Warfare: A Method," ibid., 93.
11. Ibid., 89–90.
12. Ibid., 56.
13. Paco Ignacio Taibo II, *Guevara, Also Known as Che*, 373.
14. Guevara, "The Role of a Marxist-Leninist Party," in *Che: Selected Works of Ernesto Guevara*, 108.
15. Guevara,"Against Bureaucratism," in *Che Guevara and the Cuban Revolution*, 202.
16. Guevara, "The Role of a Marxist-Leninist Party," in *Che: Selected Works of Ernesto Guevara*, 108.
17. Guevara, "What a Young Communist Should Be," in *Che Guevara and the Cuban Revolution*, 180.
18. See the next chapter, "In Search of a New Model of Socialism," in this work.
19. José Carlos Mariátegui, "Aniversario y Balance," editorial in *Amauta*, no. 17, 1928, in *Ideología y Política* (Lima: Biblioteca Amauta, 1971), 248.
20. Blas Roca, *Balance de la labor del partido desde la última Asamblea Nacional y el desarollo de la revolución* (La Habana, 1960), 42, 80, 87.

21. Procrustes was a character in Greek mythology, a warlord who invited travelers crossing his lands to spend the night in his castle. After dinner, he suggested that they sleep in the bed reserved for guests; if the unfortunate traveler was too long for the bed, his legs were cut off by soldiers; if he was too short he was stretched out by a device until he became long enough or burst apart.
22. Paz Estensoro, leader of the *Movimiento Nacionalista Revolucionario* (MNR–National Revolutionary Movement), led the 1952 revolution, but rallied to neoliberalism some years later. Rojo quoted in H. Gambini, *El Che Guevara* (Buenos Aires: Editorial Paidos, 1968), 3rd edition, 79–80. According also to Rojo: "Perón and Paz Estensoro were, for Che, examples of a bourgeoisie that, through lack of self-confidence no less than by narrowness of view and absence of historical sense, remained at the halfway point. . . ." (p. 80). We add that, in his appeal to the miners of Bolivia in 1967, Che mentions the stagnation of the Bolivian revolution of 1952 as proof that, "as regards social revolutions, there is no place for half-solutions."
23. Guevara, "Guerrilla Warfare: A Method," in *Che: Selected Works of Ernesto Guevara*, 90–91; "Political Sovereignty and Economic Independence,"ibid., 220; "Cuba: Exceptional Case or Vanguard in the Struggle against Colonialism?," ibid., 62–65; "Tactics and Strategy of the Latin American Revolution," ibid., 79–82; "Message to the Tricontinental," ibid., 174.
24. Guevara, "Cuba: Exceptional Case or Vanguard in the Struggle against Colonialism," ibid., 65.
25. See Karl Marx, *Contribution to the Critique of Hegel's Philosophy of Law*, in Karl Marx, Frederick Engels, *Collected Works*, vol. 3 (New York: International Publishers, 1975), 3–129.
26. Guevara, "Guerilla Warfare: A Method," in *Che: Selected Works of Ernesto Guevara*, 99–102.
27. Guevara, "Tactics and Strategy of the Latin American Revolution," ibid., 79; "Revolution and Underdevelopment," Speech at the Second Economic Seminar of Afro-Asian Solidarity in Algiers, February 1965, ibid., 355.
28. *Apuntes críticos a l'economía política*, 62. The Indonesian Communist Party, which had confidence in the nationalist government of Sukarno, was the victim in 1965 of a military *coup d'état* led by General Suharto, followed by its dissolution and the massacre of hundreds of thousands of communist militants, one of the most terrible bloodbaths in the history of modern socialism.
29. Guevara, *Reminiscences of the Cuban Revolutionary War* (New York: Monthly Review Press, 1968), 172.
30. Guevara, "Guerrilla Warfare: A Method," in *Che: Selected Works of Ernesto Guevara*, 95.
31. Guevara, "A New Old Che Guevara Interview," ibid., 372.
32. Guevara, *Guerrilla Warfare*, 163.
33. The Second International was founded in 1889 by the main workers' parties with the support of Friedrich Engels.
34. In 1923, Soukhanov, the Russian Menshevik Marxist historian, had written an

essay that describes Lenin's *April Theses*, a call for a socialist revolution in Russia, as a document that broke with the "elementary principles of Marxism." In a response, Lenin notes that Soukhanov and his Menshevik friends "have completely failed to understand what is decisive in Marxism, namely, its revolutionary dialectics" (V. I. Lenin, *Collected Works*, vol. 33, 476).

35. Guevara, "Socialist Planning," in *Venceremos*, 402–404.
36. Guevara, "Mensaje à los Argentinos," in *Cristianismo y Revolución* (Buenos Aires, October 1968), 22.
37. Guevara, "Guerrilla Warfare: A Method," in *Che: Selected Works of Ernesto Guevara*, 101.
38. Guevara, "Message to the Tricontinental," ibid., 179, 174.
39. Lenin's *April Theses* (1917) is the first text in which the Bolshevik leader asserts the socialist calling of the Russian Revolution. The similarity of Che's theses on the character of the revolution in Latin America and Trotsky's theory on the mutation of the democratic revolution into the socialist revolution in the colonial and semi-colonial countries is striking, all the more so since, before 1966–1967, Guevara knew nothing about the book *The Permanent Revolution* by the founder of the Red Army. That being said, it is indeed obvious that, in relation to the respective roles of the peasants and the urban proletariat, their concepts were quite distinct, if not opposed. Contrary to Trotsky, the former guerilla of the Sierra Maestra saw in the peasantry the revolutionary class *par excellence*, in Latin America and in all dependent countries.
40. Guevara "Interview with *Libération*," in George Lavan, ed., *Che Guevara Speaks* (New York: Pathfinder Press, 1967), 119.

3. IN SEARCH OF A NEW MODEL OF SOCIALISM

1. José Carlos Mariátegui, *Aniversario y Balance*, 249.
2. Published for the first time in Cuba in 1997, this letter is reproduced in the interesting work of Néstor Kohan, *Ernesto Che Guevara. Otro mundo es possible* (Buenos Aires: Nuestra America, 2003), 156–158.
3. Fernando Martínez Heredia is right to emphasize: "The incompleteness of Che's thought . . . even has positive aspects. The great thinker is there, pointing to problems and paths to follow . . . demanding his colleagues to think, study, combine practice and theory. It becomes impossible, when one really takes on his thinking, to dogmatize it and convert it into another speculative bastion and another warehouse of phrases and formulas." See "Che, el socialismo y el comunismo" in *Pensar el Che*, Centro de Estudios sobre América (Havana: Editorial José Martí, 1989), tomo II, 30. See also his book of the same title: *Che, el socialismo y el comunismo* (Havana: Premio Casa de las Américas, 1989).
4. On Che's critique of "real socialism," see Antonio Moscato's interesting study, which focuses on slightly different aspects from those examined here: "La critical al URSS e al sistema sovietico," in *Che Guevara. Cuaderni della Fondazione Ernesto Che Guevara*, no. 4, 2001, 29–50.

5. The Fourth International was founded in 1938 by left communist dissidents, partisans of Leon Trotsky, breaking with the Third International, founded in 1919 by Lenin.
6. Ernest Mandel, "Le grand débat économique," in *Partisans*, no. 37, 1967.
7. Charles Bettelheim, "Response to Paul Sweezy," December 15, 1968, in Paul M. Sweezy and Charles Bettelheim, *On the Transition to Socialism* (New York: Monthly Review Press, 1971). Also see Néstor Kohan, *Ernesto Ghe Cuevara. Otro mundo es possible*, 29 and 43.
8. Guevara, "Revolution and Underdevelopment," Speech at the Second Economic Seminar of Afro-Asian Solidarity in Algiers on February 24, 1965, in *Che: Selected Works of Ernesto Guevara*, 351–352.
9. Guevara, "Socialism and Man in Cuba," in *Che: Selected Works of Ernesto Guevara*, 159.
10. *Apuntes críticos à la Economía Política*, 372. Transcription of his discussion with Juan M. Castiñeiros on October 2, 1964. The comments of comandante Guevara during these meetings (in Spanish, "Actas de reunions efectuadas en el Ministerio de Industrias") were assembled by Orlando Borrego Díaz, a close collaborator of Che, in volume 6 of the collection *El Che en la revolución cubana*, but this document had only been selected from several hundreds of examples, reserved to Cuban leaders. Part of these debates, notably several of Che's interventions, had been published in Italian in the journal *Il Manifesto* in 1969 and translated into French under the title "Le plan et les hommes" in a volume edited by Michael Löwy in 1972: E. Che Guevara, *Oeuvres VI, Textes inédits* (Paris: Maspero, 1972). The passage cited above is found on p. 90. Large extracts appeared later in an Italian selection in two volumes: Ernesto Che Guevara, *Scriti Scelti*, ed. Roberto Massari (Roma: Erre emme, 1993). The 2006 edition, published in English translation by Ocean Press in 2008 under the title *Critical Notes on Political Economy*, while not complete, offers the widest selection to date.
11. Ibid., 11.
12. Ibid., 298–299.
13. "Collective incentives" (for example, a daycare center in a factory) or "moral incentives" (for example, voluntary work by communist militants) seemed to Guevara preferable to individual "material incentives," such as pay bonuses, without excluding the latter, however.
14. Joseph V. Stalin, *The Economic Problems of Socialism in the USSR* (Peking: Foreign Languages Press, 1972), 2, 3, 18–19.
15. Guevara, *Apuntes críticos*, 309, 332–333.
16. Ibid., 377.
17. "Interview with Maurice Zeitlin," *Che: Selected Works of Ernesto Guevara*, 391; and "An Interview with Roberto Acosta Hechevarría," in Gary Tennant, *The Hidden Pearl of the Caribbean: Trotskyism in Cuba* (London: Porcupine Press, 2000), 246. According to Roberto Acosta, Guevara had assured him that in the future, Trotskyist publications would be authorized in Cuba (p. 249).

18. Che Guevara, "Il piano e gli uomini," *Il Manifesto*, no. 7 (December 1969), 37; Oeuvres *VI, Textes inédits*, 86–87.
19. Guevara, "Socialism and Man in Cuba," in *Che: Selected Works of Ernesto Guevara*, 165.
20. Ibid., 157.
21. Ibid., 161.
22. Che used a 1963 Spanish edition.
23. This was particularly the case with two excellent works, that of Carlos Tablada, *El Pensamiento económico de Ernesto Che Guevara*, which went through thirty expanded editions since 1987 (the latest with Ruth Casa Editorial, Panama, 2005), and that of Orlando Borrego, *El camino del fuego* (La Habana: Imagen Contemporânea, 2001). On this subject, see the very pertinent comments of Antonio Moscato, *Il Che inedito. Il Guevara sconosciuto, anche a Cuba* (Roma: Edizioni Alegri, 2006).
24. This whole passage describes the contents of the edition published by Ocean Press in 2006 under the title *Apuntes críticos a la Economía Política* (to be published in English by Ocean Press in 2008 as *Critical Notes on Political Economy: A Revolutionary Humanist Approach to Marxist Economics*).
25. The New Economic Policy (NEP) was a limited opening to the capitalist market adopted by the Bolsheviks in March 1921. Janette Habel rightly observes: "Far from Stalinist deformations, Che's premises were humanist and revolutionary. But it is true that he placed too much emphasis on the economic critique, on the weight of market relations and insufficient attention to the police and repressive character of the Soviet political system." Janette Habel, preface to Michael Löwy's work *La Pensée de Che Guevara* (Paris: Syllepse, 1997), 11. Available in English as *The Marxism of Che Guevara: Philosophy, Economics, Revolutionary Warfare* (Lanham: Rowman & Littlefield, 2007). –Trans.
26. Guevara, *Apuntes críticos*, 195.
27. Feltrinelli put out an edition in 1998 under the title *Prima di morire. Appunti e notte di lettura*. Its publication in English has been announced by Ocean Press under the title *The Philosophical Notebooks: Writings on Marxism and Revolutionary Humanism*. The French edition will be published in 2008 by Mille et une nuits.
28. The *coup d'état* of Thermidor put an end to the power of the Jacobins in 1794. Leon Trotsky uses the term "Thermidor" to refer to the seizure of power by Stalin and his allies in the Bolshevik Party beginning in 1924.
29. Guevara, *Prima di morire. Appunti e notte di lettura*, 39–41.
30. Ibid., 94.

4. THE GUEVARIST HERITAGE IN LATIN AMERICA

1. Curiously, the same Jorge Castañeda, in an article published in 1997 in the American magazine *Newsweek*, began to wonder if it would really be possible to redistribute the wealth and power concentrated in the hands of elites by nonrevolutionary means, transforming the ancestral social structures in Latin

America: "We may discover, by the end of the century . . . that Che Guevara had a point, after all" (Jorge Castañeda, "Rebels without Causes," *Newsweek*, January 13, 1997). This observation, however, did not prevent him from becoming a minister in the conservative and neoliberal government of Vicente Fox.

2. Evo Morales Aima, *Pour en finir avec l'État colonial* (Paris: L'Esprit frappeur, 2006), 36.
3. We are referring here to the uprisings of Carúpano and Puerto Cabello in May–June 1962, which were quickly put down. But the survivors contributed to the founding of the *Fuerzas Armadas de Liberación Nacional* (FALN–Armed Forces of National Liberation) in 1963, headed by Douglas Bravo, which was the main guerilla movement in Venezuela.
4. In Michael Löwy, *Marxism in Latin America from 1909 to the Present: An Anthology* (Amherst, NY: Humanity Books, 1999).
5. In H. Sontag, ed., *Che Guevara und die Revolution* (Frankfurt: S. Fischer Verlag, 1968), 106.
6. The best history of armed struggle in Latin America is the work of a revolutionary Argentine exiled in Spain: Daniel Pereyra, *Del Moncada a Chiapas: Historia de la lucha armada en América Latina* (Madrid: Los libros de la catarata, 1965).

5. FROM INTERNATIONALISM TO ALTERGLOBALISM FROM THE TRICONTINENTAL TO THE INTERCONTINENTAL

1. "The Cuban revolution . . . is a revolution with humanistic characteristics. It feels solidarity with the oppressed peoples of the world. . . ." Guevara, "The Alliance for Progress," in *Che: Selected Works of Ernesto Guevara*, 275.
2. Guevara, "What a Young Communist Should Be," in *Che Guevara and the Cuban Revolution*, 184; "The Role of a Marxist-Leninist Party," in *Che: Selected Works of Ernesto Guevara*, 110.
3. "This was more than altruism on the part of the revolutionary forces, it was a pressing necessity, an imperative of military strategy in order to secure a victory of continental proportions, because there could be no partial victories, no outcome other than the total triumph or the total defeat of the revolutionary ideas. This situation in Latin America is repeated today. . . ." Guevara, "Mensaje a los Argentinos," 21.
4. Guevara, "Tactics and Strategy of the Latin American Revolution," in *Che: Selected Works of Ernesto Guevara*, 86.
5. Guevara, "Latin America as Seen from the Afro-Asian Continent," ibid,, 44.
6. Guevara, "On Solidarity with Vietnam," in *Venceremos*, 289, 291.
7. Guevara, "Revolution and Underdevelopment," Speech at Algiers, in *Che: Selected Works of Ernesto Guevara*, 350–351.
8. A thesis defended by Andrew Sinclair in *Che Guevara* (New York: Viking, 1970), 86.
9. Council for Mutual Economic Aid, a kind of Common Market for the countries

of "real socialism."

10. Even if Trotsky is never mentioned in these *Critical Notes*, one can note the analogy between this remark and the positions of the Left Communist Opposition of 1927.
11. Guevara, *Apuntes críticos*, 130, 190–191, 228.
12. Daniel Bensaïd, *Les Irréductibles. Théorèmes de la résistance à l'air du temps* (Paris: Textuel, 2001), 106.
13. Available online: http://en.wikisource.org/wiki/Charter_of_Principles_(World_Social_Forum). The authors drew their French version of this text from an appendix in a book by Bernard Cassen, *Tout a commence à Porto Alegre* (Paris: Mille et une nuits, 2003), 166. –Trans.
14. Karl Marx, *The Economic and Philosophic Manuscripts of 1844*, in Karl Marx and Friedrich Engels, *Collected Works*, vol. 3 (New York: International Publishers, 1975), 272.
15. Louise Michel, *L'Ère nouvelle* (Paris: Bibliothèque ouvrière, 1871).

APPENDIX

CHE: A THINKER OF ACTS

1. *Ernesto Che Guevara: Le Journal de Bolivie,* directed by Richard Dindo, 1994.

CONCERNING ERNESTO CHE GUEVARA

1. [This is a translation of a French translation, prepared by Laurence Villaume, from the original Spanish. –Trans.]
2. Subcomandante Marcos here alludes to the year that Che left Cuba and "disappeared" in order to assist the guerilla war in the Congo. See Paco Ignacio Taibo II, with Froilán Escobar and Félix Guerra, *El año en que estuvimos en ninguna parte* (México DF: Mortiz, 1994). [Note by French translator.]
3. Che was detained for a whole night in a classroom in the school of the village of La Higuera, before being summarily executed the next day, October 8, 1967, at the end of the morning by the Bolivian Special Forces, by order of the CIA. [Note by French translator.]
4. On October 7, 1967, Che Guevara, after having been wounded in the legs and having had his rifle destroyed by bullets (his pistol had no more ammunition), was captured while he led a detachment in the Quebrada del Yuro ravine. [Note by French translator.]

Bibliography

SELECTED WORKS BY ERNESTO CHE GUEVARA

The African Dream: The Diaries of the Revolutionary War in the Congo. Translated by Patrick Camiller. New York: Grove Press, 2001.

Back on the Road: A Journey Through Latin America. Translated by Patrick Camiller. New York: Grove Press, 2002.

The Bolivian Diary: The Authorized Edition. Melbourne: Ocean Press, 2005.

Che: Selected Works of Ernesto Guevara. Edited by Rolando E. Bonachea and Nelson P. Valdes. Cambridge, MA: The MIT Press, 1969.

Che Guevara and the Cuban Revolution: Writings and Speeches of Ernesto Che Guevara. Edited by David Deutschmann. Sydney: Pathfinder/Pacific and Asia, 1987.

Che Guevara Reader: Writings on Guerilla Strategy, Politics, and Revolution. Edited by David Deutschmann. Melbourne: Ocean Press, 2003.

Che Guevara Speaks: Selected Speeches and Writings. New York: Pathfinder Press, 2001.

Critical Notes on Political Economy: A Revolutionary Humanist Approach to Marxist Economics. Melbourne: Ocean Press, 2008.

Episodes of the Cuban Revolutionary War. New York: Pathfinder Press, 1996.

Guerilla Warfare: The Authorized Edition. Melbourne: Ocean Press, 2006.

The Motorcycle Diaries: Notes on a Latin American Journey. Melbourne: Ocean Press, 2003.

Oeuvres. 6 vols. Paris: F. Maspero, 1968–1972.

Reminiscences of the Cuban Revolutionary War: The Authorized Edition. Melbourne: Ocean Press, 2005.

Venceremos! The Speeches and Writings of Che Guevara. Edited by John Gerassi. New York: Simon and Schuster, 1968.

SELECTED WORKS ABOUT ERNESTO CHE GUEVARA

Abrassart, Loïc. *Che Guevara: Itinéraires d'un révolutionnaire*. Toulouse: Milan, 2007.

Anderson, Jon Lee. *Che Guevara: A Revolutionary Life*. New York: Grove Press, 1997.

Ariet García, María del Carmen, *El pensamiento politico de Ernesto Che Guevara*. La Habana: Ocean Press, 2007.

Benasayag, Miguel. *Che Guevara: du mythe à l'homme: aller-retour*. Paris: Bayard, 2003.

Borrego, Orlando. *El camino del fuego*. La Habana: Imagen Contemporánea, 2001.

Castañeda, Jorge. *Compañero: The Life and Death of Che Guevara*. New York: Knopf, 1997.

Cormier, Jean, with the collaboration of Alberto Granado and Hilda Gadea. *Che Guevara*. Paris: Le Rocher, 1995.

Cormier, Jean. *Che Guevara: compagnon de la révolution*. Paris: Gallimard, 1996.

Cupull, Adys and Froilan González. *La CIA contra el Che*. La Habana: Editora Política, 1992.

Debray, Régis. *La Guérilla du Che*. Paris: Éditions du Seuil, 1974.

Flavio, Koutzii and José Corrêa Leite. *Che vinte anos depois: ensaios e testemunhos*. São Paulo: Busca Vida, 1987.

Gadea, Hilda. *Che Guevara, años decisivos*. México: Aguilar, 1972.

Gambini, Hugo. *El Che Guevara*. Buenos Aires: Ed. Paidos, 1968.

Gavi, Philippe. *Che Guevara*. Paris: Éditions universitaires, 1970.

Kalfon, Pierre. *Che*. Paris: Éditions du Seuil, 1997.

Karol, K. S. *Guerillas in Power: The Course of the Cuban Revolution*. Translated by Arnold Pomerans. New York: Hill & Wang, 1970.

Kohan, Nestor. *Ernesto Che Guevara: otro mundo es possible*. Buenos Aires: Nuestra América, 2003.

Korol, Claudia. *El Che y los Argentinos*. Buenos Aires: Dialectica, 1988.

Löwy, Michael. *The Marxism of Che Guevara: Philosophy, Economics, Revolutionary Warfare*. 2nd ed. Lanham, Rowman & Littlefield, 2007.

Martínez, Fernando. *Che, el socialismo y el comunismo*. La Habana: Ediciones Casa de las Américas, 1989.

Martínez, Fernando. *Pensa el Che*. La Habana: Centro de Estudios sobre América, E. José Martí, 1989.

Massari, Roberto. *Che Guevara, pensiero e politica dell'utopia*. 5th ed. Roma: Erre emme edizioni, 1994.

Massari, Roberto, Fernando Martínez et al. *Guevara par ahoy*. La Habana: Centro de Estudios sobre América, 1994.

Moscato, Antonio. *Il Che inedito: il Guevara sconosciuto, anche a Cuba*. Roma: Edizioni Alegre, 2006.

Pierre-Charles, Philippe. *L'Héritage du Che: un point de vue antillais*. Éditions Travées, 1997.

Sinclair, Andrew. *Che Guevara*. New York: Viking, 1970.

Tablada Pérez, Carlos. *El pensamiento económico del Che: hombre y sociedad: premic extraordinario casa de las Americas 1987*. Panamá: Ruth Casa Editorial, 2005.

Taibo II, Paco Ignacio. *Guevara, Also Known as Che*. Translated by Martin Michael Roberts. New York: St. Martin's Press, 1997.

Videlier, Philippe. *L'Étoile de Che Guevara*. Vénissieux: Éditions Parole d'aube, 1997. [Text followed by "Poèmes et autres chroniques," extracts from *Verde olivo* (1959–1960) by Ernesto Che Guevara; translated from Spanish into French by Olga Barry and Pierine Piras.]

Vitale, Luis. *Che, una passion latinoamericana*. Buenos Aires: Ediciones al Frente, 1987.

OTHER WORKS CITED

Bensaïd, Daniel. *Les Irréductibles: théorèmes de la résistance à l'air du temps*. Paris: Textuel, 2001.

Blanqui Auguste. *Auguste Blanqui: textes choisis*. Paris: Éditions socials, 1971.

Borges, Jorge Luis. *The Universal History of Infamy*. Translated by Norman Thomas di Giovanni. New York: Dutton, 1972.

Castañeda, Jorge. *Utopia Unarmed: The Latin American Left after the Cold War*. New York: Vintage, 1994.

Derrida, Jacques. *Specters of Marx: The State of the Debt, the Work of Mourning, and the New International.* Translated by Peggy Kamuf. New York: Routledge, 1994.

Fanon, Frantz. *The Wretched of the Earth.* New York: Grove Press, 1968.

Gramsci, Antonio. *Selections from the Prison Notebooks of Antonio Gramsci.* Edited and translated by Quintin Hoare and Geoffrey Nowell Smith. New York: International Publishers, 1971.

Lenin, Vladimir. *Collected Works.* Moscow: Foreign Languages Publishing House; Progress Publishers, 1960.

Löwy, Michael. *Marxism in Latin America from 1909 to the Present: An Anthology.* Amherst, NY: Humanity Books, 1999.

Mariátegui, José Carlos. *Ideología y política.* Lima: Biblioteca Amauta, 1971.

Marx, Karl. *Capital.* In Karl Marx and Frederick Engels, *Collected Works*, vols. 35–37. New York: International Publishers, 1975.

Marx, Karl. *Contribution to the Critique of Hegel's Philosophy of Law.* In Karl Marx and Frederick Engels, *Collected Works*, vol. 3. New York: International Publishers, 1975.

Marx, Karl. *Economic and Philosophic Manuscripts of 1844.* In Karl Marx and Frederick Engels, *Collected Works*, vol. 3. New York: International Publishers, 1975.

Marx, Karl. *Theses on Feuerbach.* In Karl Marx and Frederick Engels, *Collected Works*, vol. 5. New York: International Publishers, 1976.

Michel, Louise. *L'Ère nouvelle.* Paris: Bibliothèque ouvrière, 1871.

Michel, Louise. *Mémoires.* Paris: Maspéro, 1976. [English translation: *The Memoirs of Louise Michel, the Red Virgin.* Edited and translated by Bullitt Lowry and Elizabeth Ellington Gunter. Alabama: University of Alabama Press, 1981.]

Mills, C. Wright. *The Marxists.* New York: Dell Publishing, 1962.

Morales Aima, Evo. *Pour en finir avec l'État colonial.* L'Esprit frappeur, 2006.

Stalin, Joseph. *The Economic Problems of Socialism in the USSR.* Peking: Foreign Languages Press, 1972.

Sweezy, Paul M. and Charles Bettelheim. *On the Transition to Socialism.* New York: Monthly Review Press, 1971.

Trotsky, Leon. *The History of the Russian Revolution.* Translated by Max Eastman. New York: Monad Press, 1980.

Trotsky, Leon. *Permanent Revolution and Results and Prospects.* New York: Pathfinder Press, 1969.

Index

Acosta Hechevarría, Roberto, 71, 130*n*17
Africa, 61, 64
agrarian reform, 50
Alarcon, Daniel (Benigno), 115
Algiers, Guevara's speech in, 113
alienation, 45
Allende, Salvador, 52
ALN (Ação Libertadora Nacional; National Liberation Action; Brazil), 85
Alonso, Aurelio, 66
alterglobalism, 99, 101, 103, 105
APRA (Alianza Popular Revolucionaria Americana; American Popular Revolutionary Alliance; Peru), 88
Arbenz, Jacobo, 14, 33, 49, 51
Argentina, 19, 86; Guevara's life in, 13–14; Guevara's message to, 94; Guevarism in, 82
Ariet García, María del Carmen, 74
armed struggle, 50–51

Bayo, Alberto, 23
Bay of Pigs invasion, 25
Benigno, 26
Benjamin, Walter, 85
Bensaïd, Daniel, 101, 111–18
Bettleheim, Charles, 67–69
Blanqui, Auguste, 42
Bloch, Ernst, 41
Bolívar, Simón, 33–34, 82
Bolivarianism, 83, 94
Bolivia, 54; guerilla war in, 94–95; Guevara in, 11–12, 15–24, 59, 113, 115; Guevara's first trip to, 14; Guevarism in, 82; revolution of 1952 in, 128*n*22; Trotskyists in, 88–89
Borrego Díaz, Orlando, 83, 130*n*10
bourgeoisie, in Cuba, 59–62
Bravo, Douglas, 84, 132*n*3
Brazil, 81, 83; Guevarism in, 85; Trotskyists in, 89
Brazilian Organization Committee, 102
bureaucratism: in Cuba, 55–57; in Soviet Union, 75

Cabello, Carúpano and Puerto, 132*n*3
capitalism, 8–9; neoliberalism and, 101–2
Castañeda, Jorge, 80, 131–32*n*1
Castiñeiros, Juan M., 130*n*10

Castro, Fidel: on Congo, 18; on economic issues, 67; Guevara and, 23, 24, 26, 29; Guevara meets, 15; imprisonment of, 14
Catholic Church, 81
Central America, 89–90
Central Intelligence Agency (CIA), 26
Chambi, Tomás, 89
Chávez, Hugo, 83
Chichina, 13
Chile, 50, 52, 83; coup in (1973), 87; Manuel Rodríguez Patriotic Front in, 81; Trotskyists in, 89
China, 113
Cienfuegos, Camilo, 23, 24
Colombia, 85, 89
Committees for the Defense of the Revolution (Comités de Defensa de la Revolución; CDR), 55
communism, 29, 32, 108; Guevara on, 37–38, 40; internationalism and, 97–98
Communist International, 96
Communist parties: Bolivian, 18, 21; French, 68; Guevara on, 35, 36; Indonesian, 128*n*28; in Latin America, 57–59, 65
Congo, Guevara in, 18, 64, 113, 115
Congress of the Organization of Latin American Solidarity (OLAS), 85
consciousness, Guevara on, 35–36
Corvalán, Luis, 87
Council for Mutual Economic Aid (CMEA), 132–33*n*9
Cuba: bourgeoisie in, 59–62; economic management in, 66–70; freedom of discussion in, 70–72; guerilla warfare in, 54; Guevara in government of, 54–57; Guevarism in, 83–84; during missile crisis, 25, 45
Cuban Revolution: influence in Latin America of, 84; legend of, 116; national bourgeoisies and, 60–62; socialism of, 62–64
Cuban Union of Young Communists, 37

Dalton, Roque, 91
Daniel, Jean, 40
Davidovitch, Lev, 75
Debray, Régis, 21–22
democracy: internationalism and, 104; in socialism, 72–73, 106
Derrida, Jacques, 100
Dindo, Richard, 115
diversity, 105

East European countries: Guevara on socialism in, 68–69; "real socialism" of, 41; *see also* Soviet Union
economic laws, 69–70
economic management, 66–70
EGP (Guerilla Army of the People, Bolivia), 19
ELN (Ejército de Liberación Nacional de Bolivia), 83, 85, 86, 88–89
El Salvador, 90–91
Engels, Frederich, 34, 128*n*33
Enríquez, Miguel, 86–88
ERP (Ejército Revolucionario del Pueblo; Revolutionary Army of the People; El Salvador), 90–91
Escalante, Aníbal, 73
Estensoro, Paz, 59, 128*n*22
Estrado, Ulises, 19
executions, 43
EZLN (Ejército Zapatista de Liberación Nacional; EZLN); *see* Zapatista Army of National Liberation

FALN (Fuerzas Armadas de Liberación Nacional; Armed Forces of National Liberation; Venezuela), 132*n*3
Fanon, Franz, 38, 39, 61
Fanon, Josie, 61
FARC (Fuerzas Armadas Revolucionarias de Colombia; Revolutionary Armed

Forces of Colombia), 89
FMLN (Frente Farabundo Martí de Liberación Nacional; Farabundo Martí National Liberation Front; El Salvador), 90
Fourth International, 89, 130*n*5
France, 9, 10, 42–43; Communist Party of, 68; Paris Commune in, 50, 57; Trotskyists in, 88
French Communist Party (PCF), 68
Frente Patriotico Manuel Rodriguez (FPMR; Manuel Rodríguez Patriotic Front; Chile), 81
FSLN (Frente Sandinista de Liberación Nacional; Sandinista National Liberation Front; Nicaragua), 90

Gadea, Hilda, 65
German Democratic Republic, 68–69
Germany: bourgeoisie in, 60; Guevara on socialism in, 68–69
globalization, 100–101
González Moscoso, Hugo, 88
Gramsci, Antonio, 46
Granado, Alberto, 12, 13, 32
Guatemala, 90; Arbenz government in, 14, 32–33, 51; *coup d'état* in, 49; failure of reformism in, 50
Guerilla Army of the People (EGP, Bolivia), 19
guerilla warfare, 52–54; after Guevara, 84–91
Guevara, Aleida (second wife), 16
Guevara, Aleidita (daughter), 16
Guevara, Celia (mother), 12
Guevara, Ernesto (father), 12
Guevara, Hilda (first wife), 15
Guevara, Hildita (daughter), 15
Guevara, María Rosario, 31
Guevara de la Serna, Ernesto "Che": Algiers speech by, 113; Bensaïd on, 111–18; in Bolivia, 11–12, 15–24; capture and execution of, 26–27; chronology of life of, 121–24; communism of, 29; early life of, in Argentina, 13–14; on freedom of discussion, 71–72; on guerilla warfare, 52–54; Guevarism and, 79–84; impact of, in contemporary Latin America, 84–91; Internationalism of, 93–96; Marcos on, 119–20; on Marx, 33–35; Marxism of, 7–8, 31, 35–37; meets Castro, 15; on missile crisis, 45; on national bourgeoisies, 59–62; in power, 54–57; pragmatism of, 47–49; on "real socialism" in Soviet Union and East Europe, 67–69, 73–74; on socialism, 40–41; on socialist democracy, 72–73; on socialist revolution, 62–64; on socialist self-management, 107; on Stalin and Stalinism, 65–66, 70, 72, 75
Guevarism, 79–84; today, 84–91; Trotskyism and, 112
Guzmán, Loyola, 15, 83

Habel, Janette, 88, 131*n*25
Hart, Armando, 66
Hart, Celia, 83
history, Guevara on role of, 35
humanism, 104

imperialism, global strategy against, 94–98
Indonesian Communist Party, 128*n*28
Integrated Revolutionary Organizations, 55
Intercontinental Meeting for Humanity and Against Neoliberalism, 98–100
Internationalism, 93–94; communism and, 97–98; in current world, 98
international trade, 93

JCR (Junta de coordinación revolucionaria; Junta for Revolutionary Coordination), 86–87
July 26th Movement (Cuba), 54

Kabila, Laurent-Désiré, 18, 64
Katari, Tupak, 82
Kautsky, Karl, 63
Kennedy, John F., 25, 45
Khrushchev, Nikita, 25, 40, 45
Kohan, Néstor, 82
Korol, Claudia, 82

Lamarca, Carlos, 85
Latin America: communist parties in, 57–59, 65; Guevarism in, 79–84; Marx on, 34; national bourgeoisies in, 59–62; socialist revolutions in, 63–64
"leftists," 36, 125–26*n*12
Lenin, V.I.: *April Theses* by, 64, 129*n*39; debate between Soukhanov and, 63, 128–29*n*34; Guevara on, 98; on "leftists," 125–26*n*12; New Economic Policy of, 74–75, 131*n*25; Third International founded by, 130*n*5
liberation movements, 99
Liberation Theology, 81, 88
Lobatón, Guillermo, 88
López, Ñico, 15
love and hatred, Guevara on, 38–39
Lumumba, Patrice, 18, 115
Luxemburg, Rosa, 42

Malcolm X, 30–31, 41
Mandel, Ernest, 67–69, 77
Manuel Rodríguez Patriotic Front (Frente Patriotico Manuel Rodriguez; FPMR; Chile), 81
Maoists, 89
Marcos, Subcomandante, 118; on Guevara, 119–20
Mariátegui, José Carlos, 42, 57, 65, 117
Marighella, Carlos, 85
Martí, José, 31, 36, 52
Martínez Heredia, Fernando, 66, 83, 129*n*3
Marucci, Peter, 55
Marx, Karl, 102; on education in socialism, 72; on German bourgeoisie, 60; Guevara on, 33–35; on socialism, 70
Marxism: Guevara's, 7–8, 31, 33–37; in Latin America, 57
Mascolo, Dionys, 114
Masetti, Jorge, 19
Mella, Julio Antonio, 57, 117
Merlino, Luis Eduardo, 89
Mesa, Carlos, 82
Mexico: Guevara in, 33; Zapatistas in, 9, 44, 80–81
Michel, Louise, 39–41, 108
Mills, C. Wright, 75
MIR (Movimiento izquierdo revolucionario; Revolutionary Left Movement; Peru), 84–85, 87–89
missile crisis, 25, 45, 94
Moïse Guevara (Bolivian guerilla group), 21
Monje, Mario, 115
Mora, Alberto, 67, 71
Morales, Evo, 82
Mosquera, Sánchez, 23
Movimento dos Trabalhadores Rurais Sem Terra (MST; Landless Rural Workers' Movement; Brazil), 81
MR-8 (Movimento Revolucionário 8 de Outubro; Revolutionary Movement 8th October; Brazil), 85

neoliberalism, 101–2
New Economic Policy (NEP), 74–75, 131*n*25
Nicaragua, 43, 89–90
NLF (National Liberation Front; Vietnam), 95

OLAS (Congress of the Organization of Latin American Solidarity), 85
Organization of Solidarity with the People of Asia, Africa, and Latin America (Tricontinental), 96–98, 114

Pacho, 16, 50–51

Paris Commune (1871), 50, 57
Pérez, Carlos Andrés, 83
Pérez, José, 88
Peru, 84–85, 88
Petrograd (Soviet Union), 62
Pinochet, Augusto, 81
planning: in economic management, 66–70; Guevara on, 72–73, 76–77
Plekhanov, George, 63
POC (Partido Operário Comunista; Communist Workers' Party; Brazil), 89
Popular Socialist Party (PSP; Cuba), 58–59
POR (Partido Obrero Revolucionario; Revolutionary Workers' Party; Bolivia), 88–89
power: governmental, 54–57; political, 48–49; taking, 49–54
Procrustes (mythical), 128*n*21
PRT-ERP (Partido Revolucionario de Trabajo-Ejército Revolucionario del Pueblo; Revolutionary Workers' Party-Revolutionary Army of the People; Argentina), 86, 87, 89
Puente Uceda, Luis de la, 84–85, 88

al-Qaida, 98

"real socialism," 10; Guevara on, 40–42, 68–69, 73–74, 97; Mandel on, 67
reformism, Guevara on, 49–50
Revolutionary Communist Youth (Jeunesse communiste révolutionnaire; France), 88
revolutions: Guevara on, 35, 37, 41–42; by liberation movements, 99; socialism of, 62–64; by stages, 57–59; violence *versus* nonviolence in, 50–51
Roca, Blas, 58–59
Rodríguez, Carlos Rafael, 67
Rojo, Ricardo, 59, 128*n*22
Russia, 57; *see also* Soviet Union
Russian Revolution, 129*n*39

Sánchez de Lozado, Gonzalo, 82
Sandinistas, 43
Santucho, Roberto, 86–88
Second International, 63, 128*n*33
self-management, 107
Sendic, Raúl, 85–87
Shining Path (Sendero Luminoso; SL: Peru), 89
Social Democrats, 35
socialism, 32, 108; of Cuban Revolution, 62–64; as cultural revolution, 40; democracy in, 72–73, 106; Guevara on, 40–41, 66, 68; Mariátegui on, 42; planning in, 76–77; self-management in, 107; *see also* "real socialism"
socialist realism (art), 72
Soukhanov, 63, 128–29*n*34
Soviet Union, 41; bureaucracy in, 56; during Cuban missile crisis, 25, 45; Guevara on, 97, 113; Guevara on Communist Parties loyal to, 35; Guevara's distance from, 65–66, 73–74; Latin American Communist Parties and, 65; New Economic Policy in, 74–75, 131*n*25
Stalin, Joseph, 40, 57, 69, 79; on economic laws, 69–70; Guevara on, 75; Mandel on, 67
Stalinism, 9; Guevara on, 72; Guevara's distance from, 66; in Latin America, 65
Suharto, 128*n*28
Sukarno, 128*n*28
Sweezy, Paul, 68

Tablada, Carlos, 83
Taibo, Paco Ignacio, II, 30
Taliban, 98
Tamayo, José María, 19, 21
Tania, 19, 20
Terán, Mario, 26
Thermidorians, 75, 131*n*28
Third International, 130*n*5

Torres, Camilo, 85, 88
trade, international, 93
Tricontinental (Organization of Solidarity with the People of Asia, Africa, and Latin America), 96–98, 114
Trotsky, Leon, 64, 133*n*10; Guevara on, 71; Guevara's quotes from, 75–76, 129*n*39, 130*n*5; on Stalin, 131*n*28
Trotskyism, 112
Trotskyists, 88–89; in Cuba, 71, 130*n*17
Tshombe, Moïse, 18
Tupamaros (Uruguay), 89

Union of Soviet Socialist Republics (USSR), *see* Soviet Union
United Fruit Company, 32
United States: during Cuban missile crisis, 25, 45; Guatemala's government overthrown by, 33; imperialism of, 96; interventions in Latin America by, 94
UNRG (Unidad Revolucionaria Nacional Guatemala; Guatemalan National Revolutionary Unity), 90
Uruguay, 83, 86, 89
utopianism, 103–4

Venezuela, 83; guerilla campaign in, 84, 132*n*3
Vietnam, 113
Vietnam War, 37, 95, 96, 117
Villalobos, Joaquín, 90–91
violence, 39; in revolutions, 50–51
Vitale, Luis, 89

women, Guevara on, 44
working class, 53–54
World Bank, 119
World Social Forums, 102–3, 105
World Trade Organization (WTO), 99

X, Malcolm, 30–31, 41

Zapatista Army of National Liberation (Ejército Zapatista de Liberación Nacional; EZLN), 9, 44, 80–81, 101, 117; on Guevara, 119–20; Intercontinental meeting called by, 98–100
Zeitlin, Maurice, 71